Contents

Preface	3
Walking with butterflies	4
Butterfly Identification	
Skippers	6
Whites	7
Hairstreaks, Coppers and Blues	8
Metalmarks and Aristocrats	10
Fritillaries	11
Browns	12

Walks

1.	Magdalen Hill Down	14
2.	Bentley Station Meadow and Lodge Inclosure	16
3.	Yew Hill	18
4.	Silchester Common and Pamber Forest	20
5.	Yateley Common	22
6.	Butter Wood	24
7.	Abbotts Wood Inclosure	26
8.	Shipton Bellinger	28
9.	Broughton Down	30
10.	Stockbridge Down	32
11.	Cowley's Copse, Bentley Wood	34
12.	Pitt Down and West Wood	36
13.	Noar Hill	38
14.	Old Winchester Hill NNR	40
15.	Butser Hill NNR and Ramsdean Down	42
16.	Whiteley Pastures	44
17.	Havant Thicket	46
18.	Portsdown Hill	48
19.	Martin Down NNR	50
20.	Pignal and Ramnor Inclosures	52
21.	Hawkhill Inclosure and Beaulieu Heath	54
22.	Walter's Copse and Newtown Meadows	56
23.	Brook, Compton and Afton Downs	58
24.	Tennyson Down	60
25.	Bonchurch Down and Wheeler's Bay	62

Butterfly flight periods	64
Check list of sites and butterflies	inside back cover

First published 2016

© Hampshire and Isle of Wight Branch Butterfly Conservation, 2016
www.hantsiow-butterflies.org.uk

Walks devised by Ashley Whitlock and Kevin Freeborn
Copyright © text by Kevin Freeborn, 2016
Photographs © Ashley Whitlock.
Except scenes on pp22, 30 and 40 © Kevin Freeborn. Back cover Brimstone, pp9 and 10 Chalkhill Blue, 13 Ringlet and Meadow Brown, 29 Blackthorn, 30 Dark Green Fritillary, 38 Cowslips and 49 Broom © Dan Powell. Scene p16 © Jayne Chapman
Maps by Kevin Freeborn, www.cartopicts.com, based on Open Street Map © Open Street Map contributors
Designed by Dan Powell. www.powellwildlifeart.com
Illustrations by Rosemary Powell
Printed by Better Printing, Southampton. www.betterprinting.co.uk

ISBN 978-0-95689-355-0

The Hampshire and Isle of Wight Branch of Butterfly Conservation is grateful to the Bentley Wood Charitable Trust, Forestry Commission England, Hampshire County Council, Hampshire and Isle of Wight Wildlife Trust, National Trust, and Natural England for maintaining the nature reserves visited in this guide and for safeguarding these very special places of wildlife interest.

The authors would like to thank Cheryl and Kelvin Richards and Juliet Bloss for checking some of the routes; and to Cheryl, Juliet and Clive Wood for their assistance in proof-reading the text.

Front cover image: Adonis Blue; Ramsdean Down from Butser Hill, *walk 15*
Back cover image: Small Blue; Tennyson Down; Brimstone

All rights reserved. No part of this publication may be reproduced or transmitted in any form or by any means, electronic or mechanical, including photocopying, recording, or any information storage or retrieval system, without prior written permission from the publisher.

This publication has been produced with care to ensure accuracy of the routes and associated information. Hampshire and Isle of Wight Branch of Butterfly Conservation cannot accept responsibility for errors, omissions and changes in the details presented. While the butterfly walks described use public rights of way, open access land and permissive paths normally open to the public, the countryside is not static and landowners may temporarily divert paths or close access for a designated period.

If you find an inaccuracy in the book, please contact **Butterfly Walks** via the Branch website.

Preface

Butterfly sightings cannot be entirely guaranteed. Seeing all 46 butterflies known to breed in Hampshire and Isle of Wight is certainly no exception. And where would the fun be if it were? But armed with this guide and given some favourable weather, and a good pinch of luck, the odds in this captivating pastime of chance should be tipped in your favour.

The walks in this guide visit 34 of the best butterfly sites across both counties. Compiled between April and September 2015, Ashley and I have walked every route – many more than once, and many of the sites are known to us from visits since the early 1980s. We have seen all the species listed for each place and there is no reason why you cannot too. On the whole these are reasonably gentle, family-friendly short walks, so pick a good weather day and enjoy an unhurried time and some splendid scenery amid the chalk downs, sandy heaths, broadleaved woodland and remnant meadows in these special places of butterfly interest across Hampshire and Isle of Wight.

One day while compiling the guide, I was wandering in Cowley's Copse (Eastern Clearing), Bentley Wood, in June, wanting to see Small Pearl-bordered Fritillary. Having no luck, I sat on a bench to take a drink and ponder the afternoon's disappointment. After a while, as I was stowing my flask back in my rucksack, two of them suddenly appeared dancing in the air beside me.

So walk slowly and patiently. Stop regularly. Let the butterflies come to you. Stay vigilant. Every now and again allow for a modicum of disappointment and, during the course of the season, this should be more than offset by the rich rewards of some beautiful butterfly moments.

Kevin Freeborn, March 2016

Walking with Butterflies

The walks described in this book follow public rights of way and/or lie across land where public access is usually permitted. Some of the routes present options for shorter circuits or longer walks. They act as an introduction to each site. Once familiar, give full rein to your natural curiosity for further exploration of other paths at each place.

Choose fine weather for going on a walk. Generally speaking, butterflies will be more active in sunny and warm conditions. On windy days seek out the more sheltered spots. As spring and summer progress, different species will be on the wing, so check the guide to adult flight periods on page 64; annual variation in adult populations is entirely typical at any site, and you may expect variation from one site to another across the region.

If you see a butterfly not on the check list (see inside back cover) please do report your sighting to the Branch at www.hantsiow-butterflies.org.uk.

Follow the countryside code (Natural England)

- Consider the local community and other people enjoying the outdoors
- Leave gates and property as you find them
- Leave no trace of your visit and take your litter home with you
- Keep dogs under effective control
- Plan ahead and be prepared
- Follow advice and local signs

Clothing and footwear
Brambles, nettles, grass cuts and insect bites – especially ticks associated with Lyme disease, found in bracken and long grass – mean that shorts are not necessarily a wise option, even on the warmest of days. Sensible footwear is always advisable.

Optical aids
Bringing binoculars has its advantages, and not just for scanning tree tops for the more elusive species such as Purple Emperor, Purple Hairstreak or Brown Hairstreak. Gaining a close-up view can aid the identification or sexing of a butterfly and can permit observation without the need to disturb it through trampling, casting a shadow or the inevitable noise of close proximity.

Photography
Photographing butterflies adds interest and challenge to a walk. Sharing the best images on the Branch website or on social media is a pleasurable and informative après-walk activity.

Records
If you don't already do it, start recording your butterfly sightings. The best method is to keep a check-list tally on each walk and then enter your observations on Living Record, see www.livingrecord.net. Once you have an account on this website you can log all your sightings for anywhere in the UK. Butterfly Conservation's county recorders are able to access this data so that your records can aid the work of the Branch and BC nationally: the more recorders and locations for which sightings are entered, the richer the data available. Try Butterfly Conservation's butterfly recording app, *iRecord Butterflies*, which is easy to use and has a gallery to aid identification.

Volunteering
Many of the sites visited in this guide are local nature reserves, dependent upon voluntary help to maintain habitats and raise funds to support conservation activities. Do please consider becoming a volunteer to help sustain these beautiful pockets of countryside. See details on the Branch website for opportunities to join work parties at Magdalen Hill Down, Yew Hill or Bentley Station Meadow. Do support other local conservation organisations, too.

Membership
Membership of Butterfly Conservation's Hampshire and Isle of Wight Branch is a vital means of supporting the work of safeguarding butterflies and their habitats. Through its various events, field trips and work parties, the Branch is working tirelessly to seek new ways to engage existing members and to recruit new ones. Do please spread the word to family, friends and colleagues and encourage them to join the branch by visiting the main Butterfly Conservation website: www.butterfly-conservation.org

Skippers

Small Skipper

Essex Skipper

Silver-spotted Skipper

Large Skipper

Dingy Skipper

Grizzled Skipper

Whites

Clouded Yellow   Brimstone

Large White   Small White

Green-veined White   Orange-tip

Hairstreaks

Green Hairstreak

Brown Hairstreak

Purple Hairstreak

White-letter Hairstreak

Coppers

Blues

Small Copper

Small Blue

Blues

Silver-studded Blue	Brown Argus

Common Blue	Chalkhill Blue

Adonis Blue	Holly Blue

Blues

Common Blue, Chalkhill Blue (top) and Adonis Blue - females

Metalmarks

Aristocrats

Duke of Burgundy

White Admiral

Purple Emperor

Red Admiral

Painted Lady   Small Tortoiseshell

Peacock   Comma

Fritillaries

Small Pearl-bordered Fritillary   Pearl-bordered Fritillary

Fritillaries

Dark Green Fritillary   Silver-washed Fritillary

Marsh Fritillary   Glanville Fritillary

Browns

Speckled Wood   Wall Brown

Marbled White | Grayling

Gatekeeper | Meadow Brown

Small Heath | Ringlet

Walk 1   Magdalen Hill Down

Owned by BC since 1989, the 'original' reserve has been extended through acquisition of adjacent land in 1997 and 2004 to create 100+ acres of magnificent chalk grassland.

A broad ridge of chalk extending east from Winchester at the western end of the South Downs, Magdalen Hill Down is a surviving piece of traditional sheep-grazed downland that once surrounded Hampshire's county town. The reserve comprises three distinct areas. There's the Original reserve, taken in between waypoints **C** and **F**, of steep-sided unimproved grassland; this was choked with scrub when BC bought the site in 1989 and tireless work since, cutting back and managing the hawthorn, has returned the hillside to flower-rich downland. The Extension lies to the east of the Original reserve and is overlooked at waypoint **A** and circumnavigated between **A** and **C**. This was ploughed and intensively farmed after World War II and its remarkable transformation by BC since 1997, patiently restored with carefully sown native wildflower seed mixes, is a conservation triumph. The carpet of yellow Cowslips is a splendid sight in spring. Magdalen Hill Down North is the third area, lying between the Original reserve and the Alresford Road, and, sown like the Extension, is being restored to wonderful flower-filled grassland habitat. In a national context this is a flagship reserve for BC.

The Walk

Cross Alresford Road and head up the track opposite passing the stonemason's yard. Go round the vehicle gate halfway up and at the top pass the reserve noticeboard (right) to reach a junction of tracks in front of a stile **(A)** overlooking the Extension part of the site.

Before the stile turn left. Walk around the perimeter of the reserve, initially with the cemetery on the left. At the end of the top section bear right with a wire fence (right) and continue to follow the reserve boundary, soon descending to the bottom corner **(B)**. Follow the boundary path as it turns right. Later, climb a stile on the right and follow a field-edge path left, gradually ascending to a line of trees ahead. Here turn right and walk up to the kissing-gate **(C)**.

Magdalen Hill Down

Go through to the Original reserve. In a few paces turn left, dipping steeply to find a crossing path emerging from the left-hand hedge. Turn right, contouring along the bottom of the down. Cross a stile and continue ahead, the main road screened by a dense hedge to the left. After a path enters the reserve from the left, the way begins to ascend to ultimately intercept a wire fence. Here turn left to reach a small stockade and a pair of kissing-gates **(D)**.

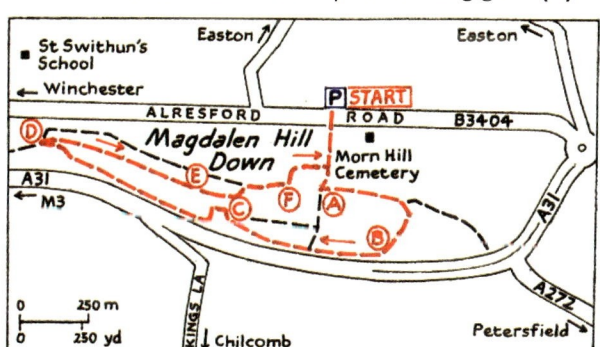

Turn right after the second gate and pass through a third kissing-gate immediately ahead, following a fence on the right. Eventually this leads to another kissing-gate **(E)**, through which take a detour along the sinuous chalk scrape to arrive at a kissing-gate giving on to a surfaced path. Turn right and walk on to a junction with a side path **(F)**, taking it left to pass two Morn Hill Camp information boards. The path curves right to reach a stile on the left. Climb it, turn right and take the grassy path to go over another stile on to the reserve access track. Go down the hill to return to the start.

Site Butterfly Conservation (BC)

Parking Parking area on Alresford Road, B3404, opposite the Morn Hill Cemetery entrance

Public transport Stagecoach services 64/65 between Winchester and Alresford stop at Morn Hill Cemetery

Distance 2¼ miles (3.7km)

Terrain Downland paths, in places steep and uneven

OS maps Landranger 185, Explorer OL32

GPS waypoints
Start SU 511 294
(A) SU 510 291
(B) SU 513 289
(C) SU 507 290
(D) SU 500 293
(E) SU 506 291
(F) SU 509 292

Refreshment Pubs and cafés in Winchester

Kidney Vetch – larval foodplant of Small Blue

Ashley's picks
Green Hairstreak – May to Jun
Common Blue – May to Jun; Aug
Brown Argus – May to Jun; Aug to Sep
Small Blue – May to Jun; Aug
Chalkhill Blue – Jul to Aug

Walk 2 — Bentley Station Meadow and Lodge Inclosure

An old wet meadow site with carr and oak woodland habitats, plus forest paths, glades and trails in the north-west corner of Alice Holt Forest.

Bentley Station Meadow is a 9-acre site purchased by BC in 1992. The nature reserve is part of a SSSI, protected for its ancient meadow and woodland fringe habitats, and lies alongside Lodge Inclosure, tucked into the top corner of Alice Holt Forest. Given its size, there's a remarkable diversity of grassland and woodland flora and fauna on the reserve, attracting 30 species of butterfly and recording more than 400 species of moth. For more information see http://www.hantsiow-butterflies.org.uk/bentley_station_meadow.php

Lodge Inclosure is an area of mixed woodland managed by the FC with popular forest trails and less-frequented paths through clearings, with sunlit displays of foxgloves in high-summer. It is also home to Alice Holt Arboretum, established during the 1950s, and now, following a period of decline and neglect since the 1980s, undergoing a programme of restoration jointly run by FC and the Alice Holt Community Forum. The restoration of the arboretum as a quiet recreational resource will benefit ecological diversity adjacent to Bentley Station Meadow SSSI.

The Shipwrights Way long-distance path (used from point **D** onwards) runs from Bentley, through Alice Holt Forest, joining Bordon, Petersfield, Havant and Portsmouth. This new 50-mile walk connects the oak forests of Alice Holt with Portsmouth Historic Dockyard, tracing the route taken by timber used for ship building from Tudor times.

The Walk

Facing the station entrance take the white-painted wooden gate in the left corner of the car park and, *with the greatest of care*, cross the railway line, turn left and pass through another white gate. Walk the tarmac path to a kissing-gate and Shipwrights Way marker stone **(A)** on the right.

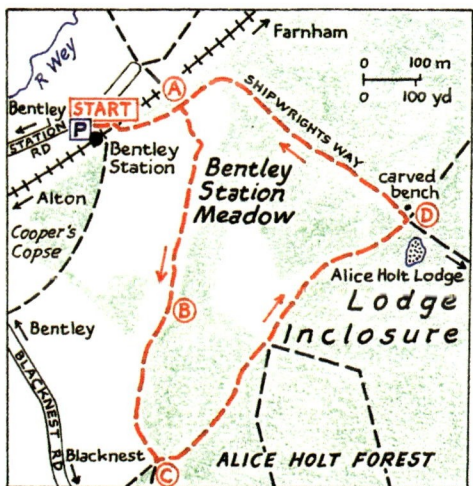

Enter the reserve. The route follows the wider and more obvious path (public footpath) running the length of the site to a vehicle entrance and kissing-gate **(B)**. To explore more of the reserve follow one or more of the narrower meadow trods, weaving around but overall heading for the southern boundary fence.

Pass through the kissing-gate **(B)** and gently descend along a wooded track. Where this opens out and there are buildings on the right, dive off to the left along a waymarked path concealed in the hedgerow. The narrow, muddy path gradually rises to a woodland crossways marked by a 4-way fingerpost **(C)**. Turn left along a wider woodland path, later emerging on to a gravel forest track. Turn left and walk to a junction of tracks **(D)** marked by a sign 'Alice Holt Arboretum' and carved wooden bench bearing the inscription *'Trees are your best antiques* A. Smith'.

Walk downhill, following the tarmac path, tracing a sweeping left-hand bend and keeping ahead past the entrance gate to Bentley Station Meadow, retracing the route to the car park.

Bentley Station Meadow & Lodge Inclosure

Site Bentley Station Meadow, Butterfly Conservation (BC); Lodge Inclosure, Forestry Commission (FC)

Parking Bentley Station car park, Pay and Display but no charge on Saturdays and Sundays

Public transport South West Trains service between Alton and Farnham

Distance 2¼ miles (3.6km)

Terrain Meadow, muddy woodland paths, forest track and tarmac path

OS maps Landranger 186, Explorer 144

GPS waypoints
Start SU 792 430
(A) SU 793 431
(B) SU 793 427
(C) SU 793 424
(D) SU 798 429

Refreshment The Star Inn and the Bull Inn, Bentley, and the Jolly Farmer, Blacknest

Cuckooflower – larval foodplant of Orange-tip. Purple Emperor - left

Ashley's picks
Green-veined White – Apr to May; Aug to Sep
Orange-tip – May
Purple Emperor - Jul
Silver-washed Fritillary – Jul to Aug
Purple Hairstreak – Jul to Aug

17

Walk 3 Yew Hill

The smallest of the Branch's three reserves, this piece of unimproved chalk grassland is managed for its downland butterflies and wildflowers.

Although pocket handkerchief-sized in comparison to other sites in the book, this open downland reserve is the epitome of pristine chalk grassland. Its variety of grasses, herbs and wildflowers, and mixture of close-cropped turf, anthills, longer grass and shelter belts of scrub and hedgerow all provide habitats for 30 species of butterfly.

On windy days early in the season the hedgerow on the bridleway side of the reserve's western boundary and the shelter along the eastern boundary are conveyor belts of spring butterflies such as Brimstone, Small Tortoiseshell, Holly Blue and Orange-tip. Running across the reserve there are several deeply rutted channels, possibly ancient cart tracks radiating south from Winchester, and these generate microclimates for chalk-loving plants and insects. The turf shimmers with Chalkhill Blues in high summer.

Beyond the entrance gate at waypoint **C** is a grass covered reservoir owned by Southern Water, not open to the public, but elms close to the adjacent bridleway are home to a small population of White-letter Hairstreak.

Yew Hill

The Walk
Begin on Old Kennels Lane at the junction with Millers Lane. Facing downhill with a thatched cottage ahead on the right, take the waymarked bridleway/access lane on the left. Where the housing ends on the left, pass a white-painted notice 'Private land' and keep ahead along the grassy field-edge bridleway with the hedgerow off to the right.

In the field corner go through a hedge gap **(A)**, beneath powerlines, and continue ahead on the gently rising bridleway until reaching the boundary fence of Yew Hill Nature Reserve. Enter the reserve by passing through the kissing-gate **(B)**.

Follow the downland path up and over the rise on the western edge of the reserve and descend to a field gate and BC noticeboard at the other end of Yew Hill **(C)**. Here turn sharp left and follow the closely-cropped turf path down the reserve's eastern flank to meet a stile in the bottom corner.

Over this turn left, uphill, and then upon reaching the kissing-gate **(B)**, bear right and retrace steps back along the bridleway to Old Kennels Lane.

Site Butterfly Conservation (BC)

Parking Roadside, with polite consideration, on Old Kennels Lane near junction with Millers Lane, Oliver's Battery

Public transport Stagecoach route 63 bus service operates an infrequent circular service between Winchester, Oliver's Battery (Old Kennels Lane) and Owslebury

Distance 1¼ miles (2km)

Terrain Easy-going downland bridleway and path

OS maps Landranger 185, Explorer OL32

GPS waypoints
Start SU 452 270
(A) SU 454 267
(B) SU 455 266
(C) SU 455 264

Refreshment Cromwell's Café, Oliver's Battery Road South, Oliver's Battery

Wild Strawberry – larval foodplant of Grizzled Skipper.
Marbled White - left

Ashley's picks
Dingy Skipper – May to Jun
Grizzled Skipper – May
Small Heath – Jun to Jul; Aug to Sep
Chalkhill Blue – Jul to Aug
Marbled White – Jul to Aug

Walk 4 — Silchester Common and Pamber Forest

Two splendid walks are linked here: one a meandering heathland ramble over Silchester Common, the other an ancient woodland wander through Pamber Forest.

Silchester Common and Pamber Forest is a SSSI, with the latter a HIOWWT reserve. They're fringed to the west and north by the villages of Tadley, Pamber Heath and Silchester, which brush the county border with Berkshire. The heathland and lightly wooded pasture of Silchester Common is a countryside heritage site, which with Tadley Common, is a surviving remnant of the formerly extensive North Hampshire heath. Pamber is a deciduous forest, mostly of oak and birch with a hazel understorey, its clearings and rides alive with butterflies in summer and home to woodland birds such as Woodcock, Treecreeper and all three UK species of woodpecker.

The Walks
Silchester Common loop

Pass through the hand-gate at the northern-most end of the lay-by and turn left along a lightly wooded path, walking parallel to Impstone Road. Reaching a hand-gate on the left **(A)**, fork right on to a narrow path and follow it to meet a broader path and bear right. Beyond a boardwalk the shingle path widens with views opening out across the heath, lightly wooded with birch, oak and rowan. Almost reaching a pair of gates, swing right **(B)**, crossing close-cropped turf. Soon join a shingle path, bearing left, and in a few strides arrive at a distinct triangle of little paths etched into the gorse, heather and ling; fork left. There are glimpses of a property to the left and then the path swings right and dips to cross a boardwalk, climbs out of the valley and continues to a T-junction. Go right to meet a drive **(C)**. Cross this and follow the path around a right-hand bend, during which it becomes enclosed with gorse. Breaking clear of this, keep ahead at a crossways. Although it wiggles around a bit, stay with this path and it leads to a view of an impressive curtain wall of mature oaks, the way dropping diagonally to plunge into the woodland **(D)**, dipping to a stream and boardwalk crossing. Do not go over it but turn left, shortly taking a boardwalk over another boggy patch. Keep ahead, taking the middle one (and widest) of three possible paths, staying under the trees. Continue to meet a prominent path descending from the left, joining it and walking right, soon crossing a rough plank bridge. Keep going to meet a track intersection **(E)**: to the left is a bridge over Silchester Brook, ahead is a HIOWWT sign at the entrance to Pamber Forest, and to the right the bridleway leads back to the parking area on Impstone Road.

Pamber Forest loop

Go through the kissing-gate at **(E)**, pass the HIO-WWT information point, cross a bridge and walk on to a junction of tracks just after a red-banded waymark '2'. Head half-right here to follow the 'Brenda Parker Way' and pass a white arrow on a red-banded post low down to the left. Stay on this clear path for about 500 yards to reach a junction with a forest drive **(F)**.

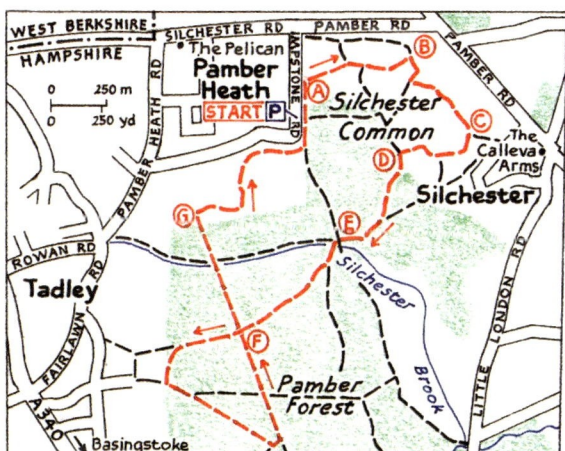

Head straight across and stay on this pleasant forest path as it sweeps to the left and emerges at a crossways. Tadley is off to the right; the walk continues left along a forest drive. In roughly 125 yards branch right along a hedge-lined grassy path. Pass red-banded waymark '4'. Meeting a shingle forest drive, turn left and then go left again at the junction ahead. This arrow-straight drive rises slightly to **(F)**. Keep going as it gently undulates its way to cross over Silchester Brook and reach a wooden barrier at the edge of the forest **(G)**. Walk out to take the path leading off right, across a playing field/meadow with the forest off to the right. Briefly walking under power cables swing left with the path, passing allotments on the right. In front of bungalows turn right and follow the field edge to reach a gap in the fence on the left. Pass through and turn right on to an enclosed path running along the back of gardens. Where it intersects a bridleway, go left to return to Impstone Road.

Silchester Common & Pamber Forest

Site Pamber Forest: Hampshire and Isle of Wight Wildlife Trust (HIOWWT)

Parking Impstone Road parking area, Pamber Heath

Public transport Stagecoach route 14 bus service between Basingstoke and Tadley stops at Pamber Heath

Distance 3¾ miles (6.1km)

Terrain Mostly flattish, heathland and woodland paths, forest drives and tracks

OS maps Landranger 175, Explorer 133

GPS waypoints
Start SU 616 621
(A) SU 616 623
(B) SU 621 623
(C) SU 623 620
(D) SU 621 620
(E) SU 618 616
(F) SU 614 612
(G) SU 612 617

Refreshment The Pelican, Silchester Road, Pamber Heath and The Calleva Arms, Pamber Road, Silchester

Honeysuckle – larval foodplant of White Admiral

Ashley's picks
Gatekeeper – Jul to Aug
Silver-studded Blue – Jul to Aug
White Admiral – Jul to Aug
Purple Hairstreak – Jul to Aug
Grayling – Aug

Walk 5 Yateley Common

Heath and woodland butterflies share the airspace here with fixed and rotary winged flying machines from Blackbushe, and delightfully aerobatic dragon and damselflies.

The Surrey heathlands stretch across the county border to this area of north-east Hampshire. Sandy tracks pass between open stretches of heather, ling and gorse while belts of birch woodland with ash and oak are found across the Common, and three ponds add to the diversity of botanical interest, insect and bird life. Silver-studded Blue, Dark Green Fritillary and Grayling are the stand-out species and Grayling, in recent years, has been recorded in better numbers on the south side of the A30. Each of the ponds is a haven for dragonflies and damselflies. Wyndham's Pool is a Monet-scape of waterlilies, Stroud Pond has a miniature pontoon for closer inspection of aquatic invertebrates and Gravel Pit Pond is fringed with reeds and reedmace. On the heathland keep an eye open for Common Lizards basking on the paths, and it is possible to see Adder, Slow-worm and Smooth Snake. The juxtaposition of heath, light woodland and ponds give rise to plenty of birdlife too.

The Walk

From the Gravel Pit Pond car park, take the footpath (*not* the track opposite the entrance) and soon glimpse the pond to the left. Follow the sandy path between the pond and a Scots pine and continue for about 500 yards to reach a crossing track and country park car park **(A)**. Keep ahead across the car park. Soon the path becomes enclosed by gorse bushes; later, in woodland, pass over two boardwalks. At a three-way fork **(B)**, take the left-hand path. At the next junction **(C)**, as you pass under power cables, fork left. Keep ahead at the crossways. Pass an old brick structure on the right and then keep left at the fork. Follow the bridleway waymark and branch left at the junction at the bottom of a sandy incline. Walk on up the incline to a crossways **(D)**. To the left is the Ely pub; the route continues to the right.

Gorse – larval foodplant of Silver-studded Blue and Green Hairstreak

Yateley Common

Look for a bridleway waymark **(E)** and follow it left. Then keep ahead at a crossways, passing into woodland – an excellent spot for Speckled Wood. Emerge from the wood on to a track with a row of houses on the right. Keep ahead but look for a path on the right just past the nearest cottage and follow it beneath trees to Wyndham's Pool (alternative start). Descend steps below the car park. Pass round the end of the lake and walk across the concrete dam. Rise to meet a bridleway waymark and follow it right, shortly breaking from the trees over open heath to reach a lane end, parking area and cemetery **(F)**. Turn right. Follow the track for about 500 yards across Silver-studded Blue country and bend to the left with it beneath power cables. Continue ahead to **(C)** and then at **(B)** go left, the path running parallel to an open field on the left. Reach an interchange of tracks **(G)** and, secreted within bushes, Stroud Pond.

Keeping the water to the right, walk around to the pontoon (submerged when water level is high). Leave the pond by completing the circumnavigation via a boardwalk and then pass a ring of logs near **(G)**, and turn uphill on the sandy track. After entering a belt of woodland the path spills out on to a broad junction a few strides up from **(A)**. Cross the immediate track and take the adjacent next left, descending gradually. Shortly, bear right on a path across the heath. This is 'Grayling alley'. Continue to reach a crossways and take the track heading off to the right **(H)**; follow this back to the Scots pine at Gravel Pit Pond and return to the car park.

Site Hampshire County Council (HCC)

Parking This site is a country park and there are several small car parks; the best two for this route are Gravel Pit Pond (second country park entrance off A30, travelling from Blackbushe) or Wyndham's Pool (off Cricket Hill Lane)

Public transport Nearest is Stagecoach Hants and Surrey route 3 bus service from Camberley with stops at Frogmore and Yateley

Distance 3¾ miles (6km)

Terrain Heathland and woodland paths and tracks

OS maps Landranger 186, Explorers 145 and 160

GPS waypoints

Start SU 838 594 (Gravel Pit Pond); alternative start SU 821 596 (Wyndham's Pool)
(A) SU 833 592
(B) SU 830 591
(C) SU 827 591
(D) SU 822 591
(E) SU 822 593
(F) SU 824 596
(G) SU 830 593
(H) SU 835 595

Refreshment The Ely, just off the route, or the Bushe Café, Blackbushe Airport, along the A30 to the west of Yateley Common

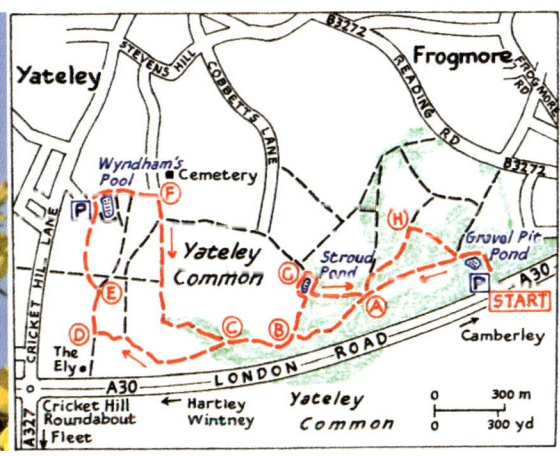

Ashley's picks
Small Tortoiseshell – Apr to May; Jul; Sep
Silver-studded Blue – Jul to Aug
Meadow Brown – Jun to Aug
Ringlet – Jul to Aug
Grayling – Aug

Walk 6 Butter Wood

This remnant of woodland pasture is a real gem, in parts jungle-like with mixed deciduous trees and a dense understorey but also with attractive meadow clearings.

Butter Wood is a SSSI (since 1986) and its 330 acres form part of HIOWWT's Bartley Heath and Warnborough Greens Nature Reserve. Part of an extensive tract of woodland pasture in centuries past, grazed by cattle and harvested for timber with hazel coppices, the old woodland management is reflected in the distribution of oak, hazel, birch, holly, ash and beech trees. On Bartley Heath, woodland has regenerated as grazing became less frequent. There are several old ponds hidden among the vegetation, their presence alerted by hawking dragonflies. 25 species of butterfly are recorded annually from Brown Argus, Small Copper, Marbled White, Meadow Brown and Ringlet along the more open rides and meadows to woodland species such as White Admiral, Silver-washed Fritillary and Purple Hairstreak.

The Walk

Just past a white-painted cottage at the end of the old lane leading off Hook Road, turn left along a grassy track into woodland and pass a metal barrier. Shortly, bear right at a waymarked fork. Keep along this track until reaching an obvious fork (waymarked) **(A)**. Bear left here but very soon reach a second waymarked fork and branch right.

Butter Wood

Noise from the M3 may filter through the trees from the right. In July and August look up at the oaks around the walk to spot Purple Hairstreak, and Purple Emperor may also be seen.

Site Hampshire and Isle of Wight Wildlife Trust (HIOWWT)

Parking Cotman's Corner, entrance to old lane off Hook Road (SU 723 523), plus lay-by along Hook Lane, between Greywell and M3 junction 5

Public transport Hook railway station is approximately 1 mile north of Butter Wood

Distance 2 miles (3.3km)

Terrain Unimproved woodland paths and tracks, some of which are narrow and overgrown and likely to be damp and muddy after wet weather

OS maps Landranger 186, Explorer 144

GPS waypoints

Start SU 723 524
(A) SU 720 525
(B) SU 713 524
(C) SU 713 519
(D) SU 714 518
(E) SU 717 518
(F) SU 718 521
(G) SU 720 523

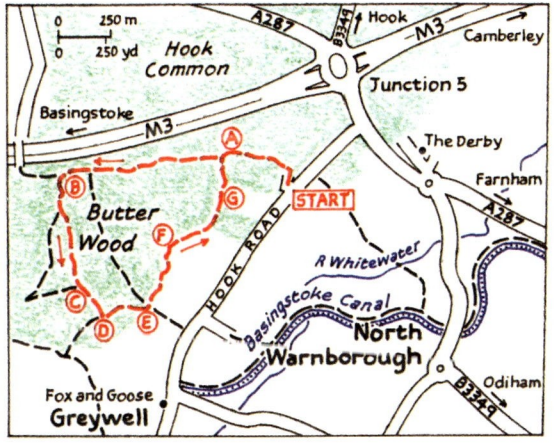

Eventually reach an old wooden hut **(B)** and just beyond swing left on to a wide ride. Farther along, a ride branches off to the left, but continue straight ahead following the waymark. Soon after, fork left (waymarked on the left side of the post). At SU 713 520, the way opens out into a beautiful meadow clearing, well worth exploring. Return to the track and walk to a five-way intersection **(C)** taking the second-left path. Continue downhill then take a right-hand fork to arrive at a squeeze-gap **(D)** giving on to an enclosed path; turn left. In a while emerge at a T-junction with a track rising up from the right **(E)**. Go left, pass through gate – 'Walkers only' sign – and wind round to the right in the direction of the waymark along an open ride. Follow the ride, keeping to the right, to a noticeable dip with a plank bridge, at a junction with another track off to the left, a site favoured by White Admiral – SU 717 520, but don't turn left, instead keep ahead to a fork at a slightly hidden waymarked post **(F)**. Stay ahead ignoring side turnings, later walking parallel with the woodland edge with glimpses of an open field off to the right. Cross a ditch **(G)** with a plank bridge on the left. Look for a waymark, bear left here, and in a short while fork right and then a few strides later reach waypoint **(A)** and go right again, following the track back to the start.

Refreshment The Fox and Goose in Greywell and the Derby Inn at Bartley Heath

Common Oak – larval foodplant - above, of Purple Hairstreak - left

Ashley's picks
Small Skipper – Jun to Aug
Purple Emperor – Jul
Purple Hairstreak – Jul to Aug
Meadow Brown – Jun to Aug
Ringlet – Jul to Aug

Walk 7 | Abbotts Wood Inclosure

Starting from a well-known Purple Emperor assembly point, the wide rides of mature oak and sallow have long made this site a stronghold for the butterfly.

Close to the Surrey border, and this book's second foray into Alice Holt Forest, the car park is an Emperor assembly point – particularly the pair of tall pines just inside the entrance gate. If visiting towards the end of June and in July and are fortunate with weather and timing, your first Purple Emperor encounter could be right here. You may well find it difficult to tear yourself away from the car park! Although Purple Emperors do occasionally descend to the ground, and perhaps alight on a car bonnet or a rucksack (if you are exceedingly lucky), get used to looking up on this walk and beware of a cricked neck. Binoculars may give you a closer view of the tree-top activity but the aerial antics and the thrill of observing chasing male Emperors may be best with the naked eye.

July is probably the best time to visit this site for White Admiral, Silver-washed Fritillary and Purple Hairstreak are on the wing. Grassland species such as Large and Small Skippers, Marbled White and Meadow Brown may be seen on open ground at the intersections of wide rides and along the verges and fringes of the woodland understorey together with Holly Blue, Comma, Speckled Wood and Gatekeeper.

Silver-washed Fritillary - above

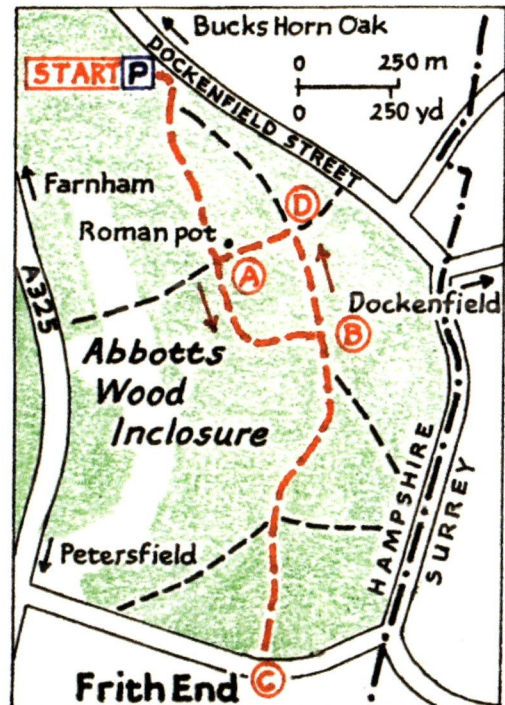

Abbotts Wood Inclosure

Site Forestry Commission (FC)

Parking Abbotts Wood Inclosure FC car park, off Dockenfield Street between Bucks Horn Oak, A325, and Batt's Corner

Public transport Stagecoach Hants and Surrey route 18 between Farnham and Haslemere stops at Bucks Horn Oak

Distance 2¼ miles (3.7km)

Terrain Mostly stony-surfaced, undulating forest drives; grassy ride (B) to (D)

OS maps Landranger 186, Explorer 145

GPS waypoints

Start SU 810 410
(A) SU 812 406
(B) SU 815 404
(C) SU 814 396
(D) SU 814 407

Refreshment The Jolly Farmer, Blacknest, and the Halfway House, Bucks Horn Oak

The Walk

Walk back along the car park drive and, just before the entrance gate, turn right on to a gated stony forest track. Follow the wide ride down to a crossways **(A)** marked, on the left, by a sculpture of a Roman pot. This is a Shipwrights Way marker stone. Keep ahead and then stay with the track as it makes a broad sweep to the left and, a little later, bends to the right at a T-junction **(B)** with a track rising to the left. Swing right and continue downhill for a there-and-back stretch to a barrier **(C)** and small off-lane parking area. En route note the major oak at a track crossing midway along on the right SU 814 400, which is another Purple Emperor assembly point. At the barrier about turn and arriving at **(B)**, walk ahead up the slope. Along the way, and before the trackside bushes obscure the view, it is worth taking a look back along the line of oaks behind and scanning the tree tops. Reaching a crossways of tracks **(D)**, turn left and walk downhill to meet the outward track at the Roman pot sculpture. Turn right and walk back to the car park.

Sallow – larval foodplant of Purple Emperor

Ashley's picks
Comma – Apr
White Admiral – Jul
Purple Emperor – Jul
Silver-washed Fritillary – Jul
Gatekeeper – Aug

Walk 8 Shipton Bellinger

The magnificent old hedgerows lining the bridleways to the west of the village offer the best chance of spotting Brown Hairstreak in Hampshire.

Shipton Bellinger is tucked into a fold of the Hampshire/Wiltshire border in the extreme north-west of the county. Backing on to land used by the military between Tidworth and Bulford Camp, the bridleways used on this walk pass through pasture, copses and unimproved open ground. This range of habitats, in addition to the lovely hedgerows, provide opportunities to spot a variety of grassland, woodland and generalist butterflies.

Thistles, knapweed, Bird's-foot Trefoil, clovers and other wildflowers line the bridleways attracting Common Blue, Brown Argus and Dark Green Fritillary while the hedges include, among other species, blackthorn, hawthorn, Wayfaring Tree, rowan, elderberry, dog rose, blackberry, ivy and traveller's joy, attracting Brimstone and Holly Blue, Gatekeeper and Speckled Wood, Small Tortoiseshell and Red Admiral and, where there are standard ash or oak trees, Brown Hairstreak.

The Walk

Take the track heading west, leading away from the road corner with the recycling bins to the left and Village Centre and children's playground to the right. The track rises gradually and after about 350 yards branch left **(A)**, on a pleasant, grassy drove parallel to the (usually) muddier bridleway.

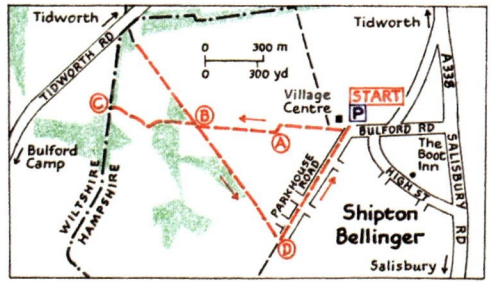

Enclosed by lovely old hedgerows and with wildflowers lining the way, this is a good, sheltered habitat for a variety of butterflies; the south facing hedge on the right is a perfect sun-trap on a fine August afternoon and, where it is punctuated every now and again by ash and oak trees, look for Brown Hairstreak activity. The hedgerows are a Holly Blue hotspot and Gatekeepers abound too, and you can see Speckled Wood, and Small Tortoiseshell in addition to grassland species such as Common Blue and Brown Argus.

Walk along the grassy byway to a T-junction **(B)**. Here you have several options: you could about turn and walk back the way you came; you could turn right and, immediately, right again and take the main bridleway back to the village; if you want to extend the walk you could dog-leg right and then left and follow the track to the Wiltshire border at **(C)**, or you could turn right and then keep ahead over the crossways for more hedge-lined wandering and chances (in August) to find Brown Hairstreak; and your final choice is to turn left, heading south-east, to return to Shipton Bellinger.

This is another pleasantly grassy track with tumbling hedgerows. After ½ mile the village comes into view and the track spills out on to Parkhouse Road **(D)**. Turn left to return to the start, passing front garden buddleias and the chance of seeing a Red Admiral, Peacock or Painted Lady en route.

Shipton Bellinger

Site Mostly on MOD-owned land, except the initial and ultimate stages of the route

Parking Car park at the Shipton Bellinger Village Centre or opposite, by the recycling bins.

Public transport Wheelers Travel route 67 bus service from Salisbury to Perham Down stops at Shipton Bellinger

Distance: 2½ miles (4km)

Terrain After a gentle rise from the start the route is generally flat and mostly on old, grassy droves; the last leg is on pavement along Parkhouse Road.

OS maps Landranger 184, Explorer 131

GPS waypoints
Start SU 229 456
(A) SU 225 456
(B) SU 221 456
(C) SU 217 457
(D) SU 225 451

Refreshment The Boot Inn, on High Street, in Shipton Bellinger

Blackthorn - above;
Brown Hairstreak - left

Ashley's picks
Brimstone – Apr to May; Aug to Sep
Speckled Wood – May to Jun; Aug to Sep
Common Blue – May to Jun; Aug to Sep
Holly Blue – Apr to May; Aug
Brown Hairstreak – Aug to Sept

Walk 9 Broughton Down

A classic north-facing chalk escarpment capped with deciduous woodland possessing a rich grassland flora, tumuli and extensive views towards Danebury Hill.

Situated about one mile south-west of Broughton this HIOWWT reserve might be accessed best on foot from the village, unless you have a 4x4 vehicle able to use the rough (and steep, if you approach along Buckholt Road from Broughton) track leading to the tree-covered top of the escarpment. Once on the reserve's open down, it is a chalk grassland paradise for calcareous-loving plants. It is a particularly good site to see Silver-spotted Skipper. In high summer Dark Green Fritillaries patrol across the down and there are resident populations of Adonis, Chalkhill and Common Blue, and Brown Argus. The old sunken drove beyond the tumulus is an afternoon suntrap and butterfly hotspot. All the while, the views to the north stretch for miles.

The Walk

Where the access track crests the hill, another track leads off to the west. Walk along this, shortly bearing right along a narrower enclosed path, which follows the summit ridge all the way along the reserve boundary and will be encountered again on subsequent stages of the route. At the next fork bear right again and walk down to a kissing-gate **(A)**, leading out on to the open down with immense views ahead. Explore this part of the slope at your own pace remembering the farther you go down the slope the more energetic the climb back up.

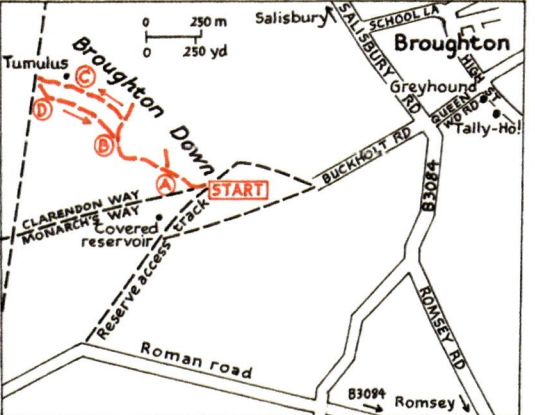

To avoid the very steepest part of the slope walk back through the kissing-gate at **(A)** and, just beyond at the path junction, go right. Walk on to pass through a kissing-gate and at a reserve information board **(B)** turn right to spill out on to the open down again. Note the grassy path contouring across the slope to the left but, before moving on, take time to see the flowers and butterflies here – in August it is a good spot for Silver-spotted Skipper.

Facing the view, drift left along the downland path to reach a kissing-gate **(C)**. Through this continue on the turf path, pass a tumulus on the right and reach a steep-sided sunken way perpendicular to the path. This bank is popular with Chalkhill Blues. Follow the path around the open meadow of the western end of the reserve and in the trees on the left-hand side find the boundary path **(D)** and walk beneath the trees with an arable field to the right all the way along the path back to the start.

Broughton Down

Site Hampshire and Isle of Wight Wildlife Trust (HIOWWT)

Parking If driving to the start of the walk, park just north of the Southern Water reservoir approximately ½ mile along the rough access track off Roman Road, where the track opens out at a crossways. If parking in Broughton, from the High Street walk along Queenwood Road, bear right along the B3084 then go left along Buckholt Road; where this ends take the middle of the three ongoing tracks.

Public transport Stagecoach route 79 bus service, circular from Andover

Distance 1¾ miles (3 km)

Terrain Woodland and downland paths, and some open down, but best to avoid the precipitously steeper slopes

OS maps Landranger 185, Explorer 131

GPS waypoints
Start SU 296 325
(A) SU 294 325
(B) SU 292 327
(C) SU 290 329
(D) SU 288 329

Refreshment The Tally Ho! and The Greyhound in Broughton

Horseshoe Vetch – larval foodplant of Adonis and Chalkhill Blues.
Dark Green Fritillary - left

Ashley's picks
Adonis Blue – May to Jun; Aug to Sep
Small Skipper – Jun to Aug
Dark Green Fritillary – Jul
Marbled White – Jul to Aug
Silver-spotted Skipper – Aug

Walk 10 Stockbridge Down

An open downland hillside owned by the National Trust, teeming with butterflies and resounding to the mellifluous cascade of Skylark song.

Passing into National Trust custodianship in 1947, Stockbridge Down is a remnant of ancient chalk grassland of wildlife and archaeological interest. The south-west corner of Woolbury hill fort runs through the top of the site and there are other prehistoric earthworks and tumuli. The down covers around 150 acres and its boundaries, satisfyingly for those appreciating geometrical pattern, are remarkably triangular. It has SSSI status, cited for its scrubland habitats, and this is carefully managed by the NT to maintain a fine balance between it thriving and encroaching upon adjacent grassland. Juniper is also found on the reserve.

Near the top of the western edge of the reserve there are long views across Stockbridge and the Test valley, bringing a sobering realisation that the down is an island site amid a huge expanse of arable farmland. 30 species of butterfly are recorded here. The areas around the hill fort ditch and rampart, across the eastern half of the site and along the sheltered bottom of the reserve, running parallel with the main road, are best for butterflies.

The Walk

With great care cross the main road and pass through one of the hand-gates. Bear half-left and, shortly, left again on to a broader turf path roughly parallel with the road, crossing the bottom of Stockbridge Down. Upon reaching the treeline in front, turn uphill keeping the boundary off to the left all the way up. Beyond a gate and stile on the left, offering far-reaching views westwards, the route climbs through wooded scrub. Keep ascending with the fence off to the left to reach a stile in the top corner of the Down **(A)**.

Here follow the grassy path round to the right to meet the ditch and rampart at the south-west corner of Woolbury hill fort. Keep forward, parallel to the ditch, and where this nears the far corner of the reserve follow the narrow trod around to the right, soon descending to intercept a broader close-cropped turf swathe. Bear left on to this and follow it into some old hazel coppice, winding gently downwards. Emerging from the trees keep ahead, walking with the boundary treeline to the left, all the way down to the bottom south-east corner of the site **(B)**. The gate in the corner leads to another car park.

Stockbridge Down

Site National Trust (NT)

Parking NT car park on the south side of the A272, about 1 mile east of Stockbridge

Public transport Stagecoach routes 68 and 77 bus services operate to Stockbridge from Winchester and Andover respectively

Distance 2¾ miles (4.5km)

Terrain Downland paths and tracks, occasionally steep and uneven

OS maps Landranger 185, Explorer 131

GPS waypoints
Start SU 374 346
(A) SU 379 353
(B) SU 387 345
(C) SU 379 346

Refreshment Pubs and cafés in Stockbridge

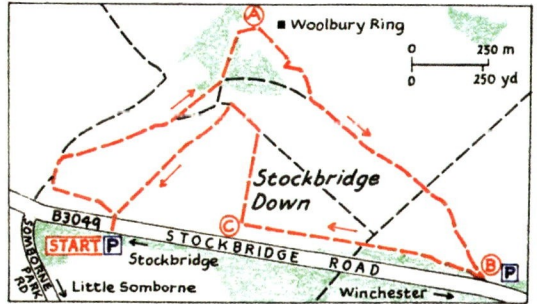

Swing right, initially walking between bushes closely hemming the path. These soon ease back and the way passes across more open downland, again with the main road off to the left. Keep ahead and watch for where the scrub on the right stops **(C)**, here turning right following the edge of the bushes uphill. Maintain direction to reach a broad path rising diagonally from the right by a ring fence of wooden hurdles. Turn left and climb to reach a gap in the gorse at the top of the hill. Turn left to pass between the gorse, staying on a broad path as it arrows its way downhill between two islands of hawthorn making a bee-line for the reserve gates. Cross the road to return to the car park.

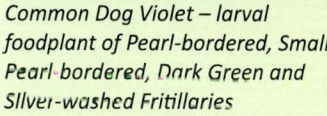

Common Dog Violet – larval foodplant of Pearl-bordered, Small Pearl-bordered, Dark Green and Silver-washed Fritillaries

Ashley's picks
Green Hairstreak – May to Jun
Orange-tip – May
Pearl-bordered Fritillary – May
White-letter Hairstreak – Jul
Silver-spotted Skipper – Aug

Walk 11 Cowley's Copse (Eastern Clearing), Bentley Wood

A number of clearings in ancient woodland connected by grassy rides managed for its trees, flora, butterflies and birdlife.

Astride the Hampshire-Wiltshire border (the car park is in fact in Wiltshire!) this 1,700-acre woodland site has been owned and managed by the Trustees of Bentley Wood since 1983. The clearings and sunny rides of Cowley's Copse, also known as Eastern Clearing, are maintained in support of a wide range of woodland flowers, including primroses, violets and bluebells, and butterflies such as Small and Pearl-bordered Fritillaries. Rotational mowing and brush-cutting around the clearings retain a varied vegetation height and structure allowing a diverse range of habitats to flourish and attracting a wide range of woodland species.

The route described here mainly follows a series of white-topped, numbered stakes but the nature of the grassy, scrubby and lightly wooded clearings means that numerous ways have been trodden through the vegetation. These can be momentarily confusing if distracted by the butterflies but it's a relatively compact site and the main paths invariable lead back to the main woodland drives.

Cowley's Copse, Bentley Wood

The Walk
From the parking area entrance go left, back along the main drive. Ignore the track almost immediately on the left, stay ahead keeping eyes peeled (for the next turning is concealed) and in about 125 yards turn left on to a well-worn trod **(A)** through the vegetation and young trees hemming the driveway. In a few strides there is a 'No horse riding' sign low down on the right and, on the left, a stake with the number '2' and an arrow on a white-painted background.

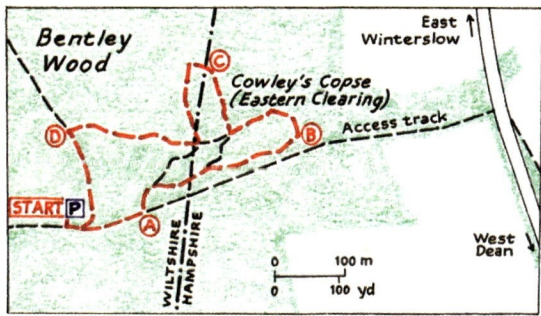

Follow the path into the clearing and soon, at a fork, branch right. Keep to the grassy trod as it follows hedgerow trees on the right. At stake '3', positioned at a T-junction of narrow trods, stay ahead. Stake '4' **(B)** is positioned in the top-right corner of the clearing. Follow the trod round to the left. Pass a substantial half-trunk bench and walk on to reach stake '5'. Here turn right across the mini plank bridge and head off on a fainter trod, passing through longer undergrowth and a nursery of young birches. The path becomes clearer and soon meets a shallow ditch and a much wider track **(C)**. Turn left and, shortly, take the next path on the left, initially crossing a little log causeway, and walk back across the clearing. Upon reaching stake '6' turn right. Soon pass a Bentley Wood information board and keep ahead to stake '7'. Beyond this emerge on to a stony forest track **(D)**, go left and walk down to pass a metal barrier and the main drive beyond. Turn right to the car park.

Site The Bentley Wood Charitable Trust

Parking Bentley Wood Visitors' Car Park, about ⅓ mile down a surfaced track off lane 1½ miles north of West Dean

Public transport West Dean station is approximately 1½ miles south of Cowley's Copse. Stagecoach route 36 bus service between Stockbridge and Winchester stops at West Dean

Distance ¾ mile (1.2km)

Terrain Rough paths and trods through woodland clearings

OS maps Landranger 184, Explorer 131

GPS waypoints
Start SU 258 291
(A) 259 291
(B) 261 292
(C) 260 293
(D) 258 292

Refreshment The Black Horse, West Tytherley

Primrose – larval foodplant of Duke of Burgundy (woodland populations). Small Pearl-bordered Fritillary - left

Ashley's picks
Brimstone – Mar to May; Aug to Oct
Grizzled Skipper – May
Duke of Burgundy – May
Pearl-bordered Fritillary – May
Small Pearl-bordered Fritillary – Jun

35

Walk 12 Pitt Down and West Wood

Adjoining tracts of downland and woodland, both on chalk just west of Winchester, offer an enticing scenario of two butterfly sites in one walk.

Farley Mount Country Park, to which Pitt Down and West Wood belong, is a large recreational amenity less than 4 miles from Winchester. Pitt Down is divided into three sections: the western part has more tree and scrub cover while the grassland is more open in the central and eastern sections, covered by this route. Grazing management in recent years has kept the vegetation shorter in the central section and there are more wildflowers here, and a good area to see Dark Green Fritillary.

West Wood is thickly wooded and, compared to some of the other woodland sites in this guide, has fewer clearings and the ride verges are more overgrown. The likeliest places to observe Purple Emperor and Silver-washed Fritillary are highlighted in the route text, but these are mobile and powerfully flying species so keep a look out around the circuit. As well as other woodland and generalist butterflies, if you are quiet enough, there's every chance of spotting Roe Deer.

A short walk option taking in both down and woodland comprises the waypoints: Start-A-B-F-C-Start.

The Walks
Pitt Down loop

Standing with your back to the lane, exit the car park via the path off to the left. Pass under tree cover and keep parallel with the lane to emerge into a car park. Walk through it, pass a kissing-gate on the right (note for later use) and keep ahead a few paces to a Farley Mount Country Park information board and kissing-gate. Go through and follow the close-cropped turf swathe, bending first to the right and then to the left before striking out across the slope. Pass in front of Forest View car park and after the path wriggles between bushes it reaches a gate at Hawthorns car park **(A)**. Here turn right and follow the downhill path, bear right at the bottom in front of West Wood and walk to the gates on either side of a crossing track **(B)**. After the second gate swing right to ascend to the kissing-gate passed earlier in the walk. Through this go left and return to Spindle Trees car park.

West Wood loop

Standing with your back to the lane seek out an enclosed path leaving the car park off to the right. Follow a wire fence (left) under the canopy to a clearing. Pass through the gateway on the left and descend into the woodland along a forest drive. At a five-way junction **(C)** turn hard right. Known to the authors as Ashley's Ride, the upcoming shallow right-hand bend is an Emperor hot-spot. Beyond the track leads to a T-junction with Crab Wood directly ahead; turn left. Walk on to arrive at a track crossing and West Wood information point **(D)**. Keep an eye out for Purple Emperors flying around the tallest oaks in the clearing. Stay on the main track, bending slightly left and then running straight for nearly ½ mile to arrive at a sweeping left-hand bend **(F)**, usually a good place for Silver-washed Fritillary. Continue, passing through dense beech woodland, which gradually eases back. In time follow the main track around another left-hander, keep ahead at a prominent crossways and eventually reach a West Wood information point **(F)**, the foot of Pitt Down visible through the trees ahead. Here you can walk forward to waypoint **(B)** and climb the down to return to the car park, or, complete the circuit of West Wood by turning left to reach waypoint **(C)**, there turning right to retrace the route out of the wood to Spindle Trees car park.

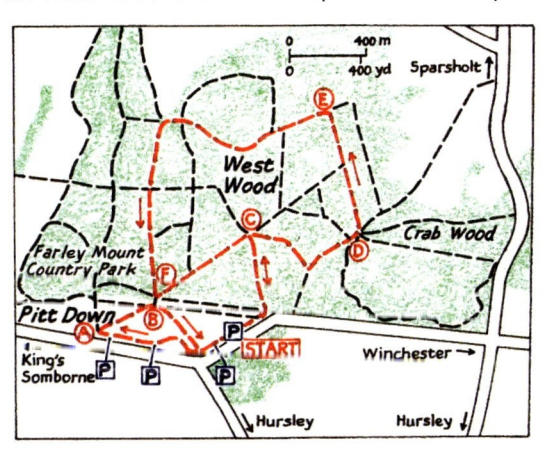

Pitt Down and West Wood

Site Pitt Down: Hampshire County Council (HCC); West Wood: Forestry Commission (FC)

Parking Spindle Trees car park; one of several Farley Mount Country Park car parks with direct access to Pitt Down

Public transport Nearest is Stagecoach route 7 bus service to Sparsholt from Winchester

Distance Pitt Down loop: 1 mile (1.6km); West Wood loop: 3¼ miles (5.2km)

Terrain Pitt Down loop: Close-cropped turf swathes across the down with a moderate descent and ascent. West Wood loop: gently undulating woodland tracks

OS maps Landranger 185, Explorer OL32

GPS waypoints
Start SU 420 292
(A) SU 414 292
(B) SU 417 293
(C) SU 421 297
(D) SU 427 297
(E) SU 425 303
(F) SU 417 294

Refreshment Nearest is the Plough Inn, Sparsholt

Thistle species – larval foodplants of Painted Lady - left

Ashley's picks
Small Skipper – Jun to Aug
Large Skipper – Jun to Aug
Dark Green Fritillary – Jul
Marbled White – Jul to Aug
Silver-washed Fritillary – Jul to Aug

Walk 13 Noar Hill

Long-abandoned, ancient chalk workings form a wildflower-rich grassland of hummocks and hollows with Juniper and mature broadleaved woodland.

Managed by HIOWWT, the site is a SSSI and has been a nature reserve since 1982, maintained for its chalk grassland flora and fauna. High Common, the area of Noar Hill where chalk was dug from medieval times, is a landscape of sheltered scoops and sun-trap scrapes that, due to the quarrying activity, has never been ploughed. Patches of exposed chalk, thin calcareous soil, the variety of aspect, slope steepness and irregular terrain created by the old workings all give rise to a range of niches for plants and insects, especially orchids and butterflies.

The microclimates created in the shelter of the chalky hollows are great for wildflowers and butterflies, so do divert off the described route, but keep to the existing side-paths and *be especially careful not to trample wildflowers when walking on the reserve.*

An apron of mature woodland, known in these parts as 'hangers' and visited by the Hangers Way long-distance path, curls round the slopes of Noar Hill. The hanger fringes are a good place to spot woodland butterflies and patches of shrubby scrubland mixed with longer grassland provide an excellent mix of butterfly habitats.

Noar Hill

The Walk

Walk along the waymarked bridleway and Charity Farm access track. In about 100 yards, branch left along a narrower waymarked path to reach a hand-gate and Noar Hill Nature Reserve sign **(A)**. Enter the reserve. A site of old chalk workings, there are several possibilities to venture along side-paths in successive hollows and scrapes, well worth exploring, but the directions given here follow the main track to waypoint **(D)** before inviting you to pick a return path to the reserve entrance at **(A)**.

Keep ahead along the main path, rising all the while and later moving beneath tree cover. Maintain direction past a three-way fingerpost and gradually ascend to a splendid viewpoint and well-appointed bench **(B)**.

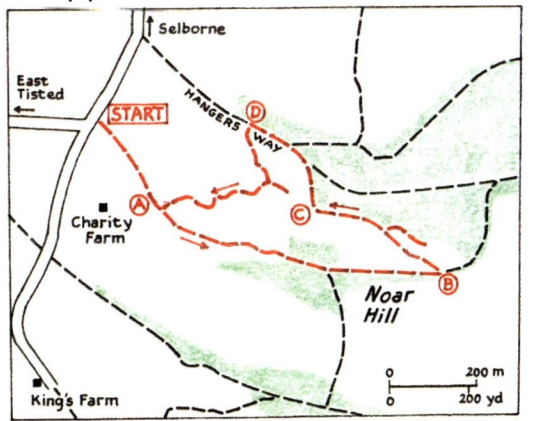

Swing sharp left keeping a deeply-scooped hollow on the right. Stay with the main track walking gently downhill to reach a reserve information board **(C)**. Bear right here, descending to a hand- and field-gate combination. Through the gate ease left on to a broad track – The Hangers Way – and walk down to a kissing-gate **(D)**, on the left, giving access back on to the reserve.

Follow the obvious rising trod, which weaves a way up the slope. At the top, thread a way from one grassy trod to another, heading in the general direction of the barn rooftops of Charity Farm when these come into view, crossing the reserve to arrive back on the outbound track close to **(A)**. Pass through the hand-gate and walk down to the lane.

Site Hampshire and Isle of Wight Wildlife Trust (HIOWWT)

Parking Verge parking with polite consideration – *avoid blocking farm access* – by Charity Farm on lane south of Selborne

Public transport Stagecoach route 38 bus service between Alton and Petersfield to Selborne

Distance 2 miles (3.2km)

Terrain Grassland paths and tracks with moderate rises and descents.

OS maps Landranger 186, Explorer OL33

GPS waypoints
Start SU 737 321
(A) SU 738 319
(B) SU 745 317
(C) SU 742 319
(D) SU 740 321

Refreshment The Selborne Arms and The Queens Head in Selborne; The Selborne Tea Room and the Tea Parlour at Gilbert White's House, Selborne

Cowslip – larval foodplant of Duke of Burgundy - left.
Duke of Burgundy - left

Ashley's picks
Duke of Burgundy – May
Brown Argus – May to Jun; Aug to Sep
Small Heath – Jun; Aug to Sep
Essex Skipper – Jul to Aug
Brown Hairstreak – Aug to Sep

Walk 14 Old Winchester Hill NNR

A steep-sided, wildflower-rich chalk downland with a prominent Iron Age hill fort and deciduous and yew woodland.

A prominent chalk eminence, Old Winchester Hill has commanding views the length of the Meon valley to the silver ribbon of The Solent and Isle of Wight. The site is rich in archaeological and historical interest with Neolithic flint implements having been found on the hill, Bronze Age tumuli, a crowning Iron Age hill fort and it was used by the military as a mortar range during World War II. Botanically there are several nationally important species including Juniper, Round-headed Rampion, and a number of downland orchids, as well as Small and Devil's-bit Scabious and Autumn Lady's Tresses. Popular, too, with ornithologists the site attracts farmland, grassland and woodland species and is an important stopover for migratory species. Kestrels are a familiar sight hovering above the hill fort. The South Downs Way and Monarch's Way long-distance paths thread their way around the NNR.

The reserve records 37 species of butterfly and the South Slope is prime chalk grassland habitat. Here larval foodplants such as Horseshoe Vetch, Kidney Vetch and Bird's-foot Trefoil are widespread and in July and August there are shimmering clouds of Chalkhill Blues.

The Walk

Use the hand-gate from the car park to access the reserve. In a few steps fork left and stride out along the top of the down with exceptional views off to the right over the hill fort and the Meon valley. Approaching a boundary fence, a stony access track crosses from the left. Join it, walk right, pass through a gateway gap **(A)** and stay on the main track to a metal kissing-gate/vehicle-gate **(B)**.

Old Winchester Hill NNR

There's a South Downs Way (SDW) fingerpost here and the hill fort lies ahead. Through the kissing-gate swing left in front of the ramparts and stay on the lower path as it follows the perimeter fence (left) around to a field-gate gap **(C)** at the top of the reserve's south slope. Through this, follow the path diagonally right, down the hill all the way to a kissing-gate and reserve noticeboard **(D)** at the bottom.

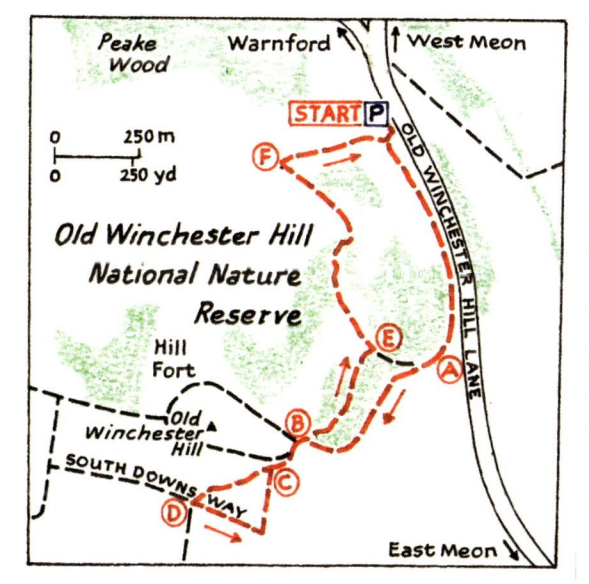

Site Natural England (NE)

Parking NNR car park

Public transport Nearest bus service is between Winchester and Petersfield and stops at West Meon and East Meon

Distance 2½ miles (3.9km)

Terrain Downland paths and tracks, in places steep and uneven

OS maps Landranger 185, Explorer OL3

GPS waypoints
Start SU 645 214
(A) SU 647 207
(B) SU 643 205
(C) SU 642 204
(D) SU 640 203
(E) SU 645 208
(F) SU 642 213

Refreshment The Shoe at Exton, the George and Falcon at Warnford and the Thomas Lord at West Meon

Beyond the gate go left and walk along the field-edge path to the next SDW fingerpost. Here turn uphill following the SDW with the reserve to the left and a vineyard to the right. Follow the SDW through a hand-gate to return to **(B)**. Go through the metal kissing-gate and then turn right, down steps and follow the path contouring around the hillside until reaching a T-junction **(E)** just below a field-gate (right). Turn left, descending very steeply to enter woodland through a kissing-gate at the bottom. After winding through trees reach a kissing-gate and keep ahead with the ongoing chalk path. Where this suddenly stops **(F)** turn right on to a close-cropped turf path for the haul back up to the car park, gained by passing through a kissing-gate at the top of the slope then keeping ahead on the main path to the reserve gate.

Sheep's Fescue – larval foodplant of Gatekeeper

Ashley's picks
Common Blue – May to Jun; Aug to Sep
Small Copper – May; Jul to Aug
Large Skipper – Jun to Aug
Chalkhill Blue – Jul to Aug
Silver-spotted Skipper – Aug

Walk 15 — Butser Hill NNR and Ramsdean Down

Butser's smoothly and curvaceously rounded bulk conceals within its downland folds a sheltered and close-cropped turf paradise for grassland butterflies.

⚠️ This walk crosses steep slopes and may present difficulties for vertigo sufferers.

Butser Hill is the highest point on the South Downs at 270m (885ft) above sea level. Its radio communications tower is a landmark along the A3 corridor and there are far-reaching panoramic views: southwards across The Solent to the Isle of Wight, the Meon valley and beyond to the west, northwards overlooking Petersfield, and to the east the dips and rises of the South Downs extend far into Sussex. It lies within the Queen Elizabeth Country Park, managed by HCC for a very wide range of recreational, educational and natural history interests.

The western coombe, around which this walk is based, is a spectacularly steep-sided dry valley. The upper, more exposed parts of the walk are likely to be breezy, even on the best of days, while it can feel like a different world in the valley bottom protected by the sheltering arm of Ramsdean Down. Most of the walk is over open grassland but there are patches of scrub and hedgerow trees near the bottom of Ramsdean Down. Take it easy on the stiff climb at the end of the route – hopefully there will be a multitude of butterfly distractions and the ascent will be over before you know it.

Butser Hill NNR & Ramsdean Down

Site Hampshire County Council (HCC) and Natural England (NE)

Parking Butser Hill car park (Pay and Display)

Public transport Stagecoach route 37 bus service between Petersfield and Havant to Queen Elizabeth Country Park visitor centre

Distance 1¾ miles (2.7km)

Terrain Downland paths, sometimes uneven and, near the end of the walk, breathtakingly steep (literally!)

OS maps Landranger 197, Explorer OL8

GPS waypoints
Start SU 711 200
(A) SU 712 203
(B) SU 709 207
(C) SU 709 209
(D) SU 709 206

Refreshment The Queen Elizabeth Country Park visitor centre café

Bird's-foot Trefoil – larval foodplant of Dingy Skipper and Common Blue. Grizzled Skipper - left

Ashley's picks
Dingy Skipper – May to Jun
Grizzled Skipper – May
Green Hairstreak – May to Jun
Duke of Burgundy – May
Small Heath – Jun; Aug to Sep

The Walk

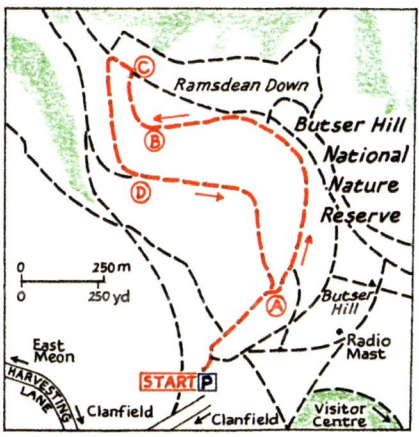

Walk to the far (north) end of the car park to pick up a path through scrub, which then ducks down beneath yew trees to reach a kissing-gate. Go through and take an ascending grassy trod on the right, aiming for a gap in the bushes at the top of the hill. Over the crest, the radio communications tower stands to the right, walk with a fence on the right past a kissing-gate. The way starts to dip, the descent becoming increasingly steep through scrub, leading to a path junction **(A)**.

Fork right here on to a bold chalk path that contours around the head of the impressive natural amphitheatre. Later on, ignore steps and stay on the obvious path as it curves left on to the ridge of Ramsdean Down. Gradually the narrow contour path widens to a close-cropped turf swathe descending the ridge, with the spire of East Meon church ahead in the distance.

Lower down at a path junction **(B)** fork right and follow the grassy trod with the land falling away more steeply to the left. Picking a way through a patch of scrub, meet a broader path sweeping down from the right **(C)** and turn left. This path descends to a crossways. Turn left and follow a narrow path worn into the chalk, gradually descending, and later curving gently left to meet a clump of grand beeches in the bottom of the dry valley **(D)**.

Turn left along the valley bottom path and walk towards the looming bulk of Butser. After curving right climb exceptionally steeply to return to **(A)**; from here retrace the route to the car park.

43

Walk 16 Whiteley Pastures

An opportunity to combine a good butterfly walk with some retail therapy or, perhaps, an excuse to duck out of the shopping and have a woodland wander.

Despite its name this is an ancient woodland site and SSSI, once part of the extensive medieval Forest of Bere stretching from Sussex across southern Hampshire to the New Forest. This former tract of productive coppice and native deciduous species (particularly oak) with woodland grazing is now rather overgrown and evidence of the open nature of the wooded pasture is increasingly lost; but, with bordering Botley Wood, it is still a good site for some woodland butterflies and commoner grassland species along the rides. Thistles and occasional buddleia dotted along the rides attract Peacock, Red Admiral, Painted Lady and Comma, nectaring alongside Silver-washed Fritillary, while Gatekeeper, Meadow Brown, Ringlet, Speckled Wood and Large and Small Skippers flit along the woodland verges. While, sadly, Brown Hairstreak, Marsh and Pearl-bordered Fritillary may no longer be seen, don't be put off by the proximity of modern housing, business and retail development; this is still a wonderful woodland for Roe Deer, birds and butterflies.

The Walk

Make your way from the car parks to cross Marjoram Way and follow the pavement at the roundabout to use the pedestrian crossing on Whiteley Way. Bear slightly right and continue ahead on the surfaced path with your back to Whiteley Way, walking with the 'Zurich' building to the right and willows, alders and a pond to the left. The footpath bends sharply left and then right, leading to a junction with a stony track. Turn left along it and then follow it round to the right to a barrier and Whiteley Pastures information board **(A)**.

Keep ahead on this oak-lined main ride, in July scanning the tree tops for oak-edging Purple Emperor. After approximately 450 yards go left **(B)** along a narrower ride, the track becoming increasingly grass covered. Along this ride all life appears to be confined to the corridor of woodland fringe and wildflower verges, such is the darkness of the density of trees in the adjacent plantations. Look out for dragonflies and damselflies at the pond on the right-hand side (SU 534 103).

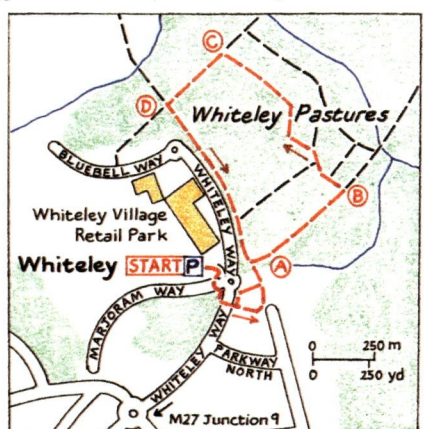

At a track crossways **(C)**, watch for Purple Hairstreak at the oaks here. Go left along the arrow-straight track for approximately 275 yards to the next crossways **(D)**, a noted corner for White Admiral. Turn left here, the trees on the right gradually thinning adjacent to the Retail Park. Keep ahead to a T-junction to regain the main ride and retrace your outbound steps to a footbridge on the right, cross it and follow the surfaced path to the pedestrian crossing over Whiteley Way.

Whiteley Pastures

Site Forestry Commission (FC)

Parking One of the public car parks off Marjoram Way at Whiteley Retail Park; parking is free for up to 3 hours

Public transport First Group route 28A/28 bus services to Whiteley Retail Park from Fareham

Distance 2¼ miles (3.5km)

Terrain A flat route along woodland rides and tracks which, depending upon forestry operations, can be muddy after wet weather

OS maps Landranger 196, Explorer OL3

GPS waypoints
Start SU 532 096
(A) SU 534 096
(B) SU 537 099
(C) SU 532 104
(D) SU 530 102

Refreshment A number of options exist at Whiteley Retail Park

Holly; Ivy – larval foodplants of Holly Blue (spring and summer broods respectively). White Admiral - left

Ashley's picks
Holly Blue – Apr to May; Aug
Comma – Apr; Jul; Sep
White Admiral – Jul to Aug
Silver-washed Fritillary – Jul to Aug
Ringlet – Jul to Aug

45

Walk 17 Havant Thicket

Attractive forest with broad rides and a profusion of wildflowers along track-side verges making it a good site for woodland and grassland butterflies.

Good access and generally well-made tracks and paths combine to make this route an ideal walk for a family afternoon out. The paths are mostly level or gently undulating and benches can be found along the way. Bring a picnic to enjoy. And don't forget binoculars, which might be helpful for scanning the oak-tops for the regal Emperor.

Undisputedly a woodland site, its mixed stands of mature oak and sallow make it prime Purple Emperor habitat. Although for those making their first visit in summer there's an unexpected attractiveness in the number of wildflowers and grassland butterflies found along the wide rides, including Large and Small Skipper, Common Blue, Marbled White and Meadow Brown. Add to this Brimstone and generalist species such as Red Admiral, Peacock, Small Tortoiseshell, Comma and the Whites and you can build up quite an impressive checklist for the site before including woodland species such as Purple Emperor, White Admiral, Silver-washed Fritillary and Speckled Wood, and hedgerow-lovers like Gatekeeper and Ringlet.

Havant Thicket

The Walk

From the sturdy information point head along the path leading from the car park. Shortly, at a T-junction of paths, turn right and walk along an arrow-straight track for almost ½ mile to another T-junction **(A)** deeper in the woods. Turn left and stay on this pleasant, stony forest track, ignoring all perpendicular offshoot paths, for ¾ mile. Look out for a shallow dip in the track, lined by mature oaks: Purple Emperors are seen here annually and the last and largest of these trees on the right is particularly favoured by the male butterflies. Eventually arrive at a T-junction **(B)** in a wide intersection of rides. In front lies Bell's Copse and to the left there's an information board about the reservoir proposed for this site and the adjacent land, but the walk continues to the right along another straight forest track.

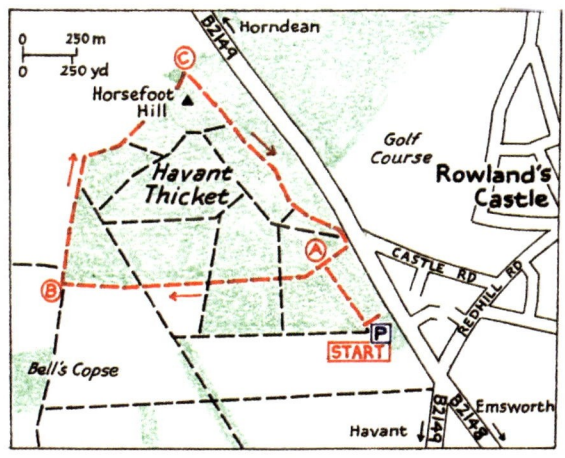

Site Forestry Commission (FC)

Parking Havant Thicket car park, signed as the 'Forest of Bere' off B2149, north of Havant and west of Rowland's Castle

Public transport Rowland's Castle station is approximately 1 mile east of Havant Thicket

Distance 3 miles (4.7km)

Terrain Reasonably level, surfaced or improved tracks and paths; good for pushchairs and wheelchairs

OS maps Landranger 197, Explorer OL8

GPS waypoints
Start SU 723 102
(A) SU 720 104
(B) SU 708 103
(C) SU 714 113

Refreshment The Robin Hood Inn or the Castle Inn in Rowland's Castle

Stay on the track round a right-hand bend and keep ahead, with glimpses of open fields through the trees on the left, rising almost imperceptibly to reach a corner **(C)** in pretty much the northern-most point of Havant Thicket. This is Horsefoot Hill and the clearing here in the canopy is a well-known Emperor assembly point. Turn right with the track and, later on, meet a gated vehicle entrance leading to the Rowland's Castle road. Stay with the main track as it swings right and in about 350 yards reach waypoint **(A)**. Here go left and simply retrace the outward route back to the car park.

Stinging Nettle – larval foodplant of Small Tortoiseshell, Peacock, Red Admiral and Comma. Gatekeeper - left

Ashley's picks
Painted Lady – Apr to Sep
White Admiral – Jul to Aug
Purple Emperor – Jul
Silver-washed Fritillary – Jul to Aug
Gatekeeper – July to Aug

Walk 18 Portsdown Hill

A magnificent, lengthy spine of chalk grassland whose south-facing slopes present stunning views across Portsmouth Harbour to the Isle of Wight.

This is an extensive chalk grassland nature reserve seemingly only a stone's throw from the urban centres of Portsmouth, Gosport and Fareham. There is a network of paths across the site with plenty of opportunity to divert from the suggested route to see the wildflowers, butterflies and watch the birdlife. The top path taken on the way out has the sanctuary of hedgerow shelter, sometimes enclosing the path on both sides, but punctuated with open, grassy sun-traps and possessing a great variety of vegetation heights. Holly Blue, Speckled Wood, Brimstone, all the common whites, Red Admiral, Peacock, Small Tortoiseshell and Comma are all found here along with Green Hairstreak, Small Blue, Marbled White, Meadow Brown and Gatekeeper. The proximity of gardens at the bottom of the slope make it an attractive site for cabbage whites and other garden visitors. Chalkhill Blues love the open, south-facing down. Violets are increasing on the site and Dark Green Fritillary is being recorded once again. The western half of the down tends to see higher butterfly numbers. Much of Portsdown has SSSI status and the site is managed by Portsmouth City Council and Natural England. The close proximity of the Victorian forts may tempt history lovers to take in a military museum or two.

Portsdown Hill

The Walk
Facing the sea view leave the car park opposite its entrance down a grassy bank, *carefully* cross the road (James Callaghan Drive) and walk through the roadside vegetation to a clear pathway running parallel to and just below the road. Turn right.

There are several opportunities to pass on to the open downland via stiles, gates and gaps in the hedge should you wish to wander independently but this route follows the top path for just under a mile (1.5km), eventually reaching a stile **(A)** on the left. Cross over, walk down the slope a few strides and pick up a crossing path, going right. You are now walking above the old quarry whose prominent chalk cliff is seen from the M27. Pass through a metal kissing-gate and fork left walking diagonally downhill. Near the bottom bear right with the path, pass a towering pylon and then walk in the direction of the overhead cables. Later, the path begins to climb, passing under the powerline. Soon on the left there's an overgrown fence topped with barbed-wire; here look for a path climbing diagonally right. Stay on this to reach a tarmac lane **(B)**. Turn uphill along it, follow it round to the right, go through a wooden kissing-gate in the left-hand hedge and walk up to the road, turning right along the verge.

Just beyond a mini-roundabout fork right from the verge along a cleared path and walk below but parallel to the road to regain the stile **(A)**, now on the right. Hop over and descend to the crossing path, this time going left. Keep ahead until there is a pronounced ditch; descend and rise via wooden steps to a redundant metal gateway **(C)**. Beyond, maintain direction by forking, first, left and, later, right to meet a chalky crossways **(D)** turning left, initially quite steeply, up a deeply rutted path. Climb to branch right along a path, once again parallel to the road off to the left. The path leads back to the start: the overhead power cable is a useful marker for the car park.

Site Portsmouth City Council

Parking James Callaghan roundabout car park off B2177, west of Fort Widley

Public transport First Group service 7C runs along Portsdown Hill Road

Distance 3¼ miles (5.2km)

Terrain Grassland paths with moderate rises and descents, verges and surfaced path.

OS maps Landranger 196, Explorer OL3

GPS waypoints
Start SU 647 066
(A) SU 632 067
(B) SU 626 067
(C) SU 638 066
(D) SU 640 065

Refreshment The viewpoint car park hosts a burger and hotdog vendor and there's often an ice cream van as well: options, then, for main course and dessert!

Orange-tip female - above.
Broom – larval foodplant of Green Hairstreak - top

Ashley's picks
Small White – May; Jul to Sep
Small Blue – May to Jun; Aug
Green Hairstreak – May to Jun
Red Admiral – Apr to May; Jul to Oct
Marbled White – Jul to Aug

Walk 19 Martin Down NNR

An extensive area of chalk grassland in the far west of the county where Dorset, Wiltshire and Hampshire meet.

There is definitely a sense of space, perhaps even an air of remoteness, to Martin Down and, with just a little imagination, there's also a touch of Great Plains' grassland about the site. It's a large nature reserve, but its 336 hectares are only a surviving fragment of the former chalk grasslands of Southern England. Under a canopy of wide blue sky and a mellifluous cascade of Skylark song, a butterfly walk here is as peaceful and 'away from it all' as it is possible to get in Hampshire.

The micro-climate and botanical diversity of the ditch and bank of Bokerley Ditch attract a range of butterfly species, which is why much of the walk follows this ancient earthwork. The former rifle range, with its close-cropped turf and the thin soil of its steep banks, is another area worth closer investigation. In the more open areas of the reserve, look for the shelter afforded by scrub and path-side vegetation as good places to see butterflies, especially on a windy day.

The Walk

In the car park, with your back towards the vehicle entrance, walk to the far end and pass through the gap by a locked barrier to the right of a trio of reserve information boards. Keep ahead through a patch of scrub and maintain direction across the grassland, roughly parallel to the main road and reserve hedge-line 50 yards or so away to the right. Upon reaching the ancient earthwork of Bokerley Ditch **(A)** turn left.

The route now simply follows Bokerley Ditch, which also marks the Dorset-Hampshire county boundary, keeping the ditch and bank to the right. Pass two prominent banks (a former rifle range), running perpendicular to Bokerley Ditch away to the left, and eventually reach a reserve signpost and crossing public path **(B)**. Here turn left along the chalky way, heading eastward across the reserve, or choose to extend the walk farther alongside Bokerley Ditch and then retrace steps to **(B)**, there turning right.

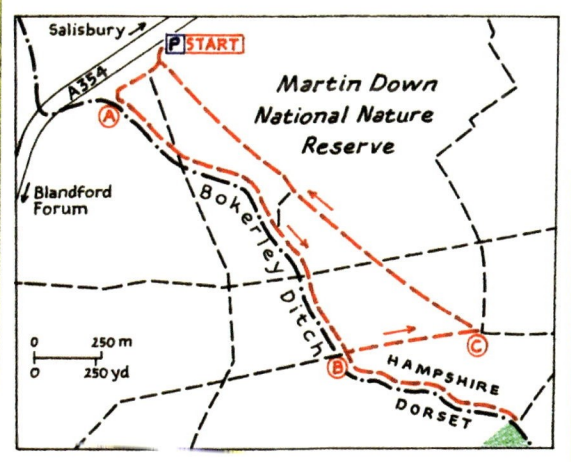

At a five-way track junction on the other side of the reserve **(C)** turn sharply to take the first track left. Follow this straight grassy vehicle track, eventually passing the opposite ends of the high banks of the former rifle range encountered earlier in the walk. Keep ahead as the track becomes stony and return to the car park.

Martin Down NNR

Site Hampshire County Council (HCC) and Natural England (NE)

Parking NE car park on the eastern side of the A354 between Woodyates and Martin Drove End

Public transport Wilts and Dorset Bus Company route X12 service from Salisbury and, less frequently, services 314 and 400; nearest stop on A354 by the car park entrance

Distance 3½ miles (5.7km)

Terrain Reasonably level grassy paths and tracks

OS maps Landranger 184, Explorer 118

GPS waypoints
Start SU 036 200
(A) SU 035 199
(B) SU 043 189
(C) SU 048 190

Refreshment The Rose and Thistle at Rockbourne or The Queens Head at Broad Chalke

Devil's-bit Scabious – larval foodplant of Marsh Fritillary; Marsh Fritillary - left

Ashley's picks
Marsh Fritillary – May to Jun
Adonis Blue – May to Jun; Aug to Sep
Small Blue – May to Jun; Aug
Brown Argus – May to Jun; Aug to Sep
Dark Green Fritillary – Jul

51

Walk 20 Pignal and Ramnor Inclosures

Woodland glades and rides, track verges and New Forest trails with stands of broadleaved and coniferous trees to the north-east of Brockenhurst.

Tucked away behind the Balmer Lawn Hotel, off the A337 just north of Brockenhurst, Standing Hat is reached via a long gravelled forest drive. The main – gravel-surfaced – forest trails are dedicated cycle ways, popular at weekends and holiday periods so beware of speeding bicycles. Along the quieter tracks there are grassy rides and recent forestry operations have opened clearings, which are favoured spots for Pearl-bordered Fritillary. Trackside drainage ditches attract dragonflies and damselflies, Jays and Great Spotted Woodpeckers add avian interest and on spring mornings the air is filled with woodland birdsong.

The Walk
Bear left from the car park entrance to pass through the hand-gate, and take the left-hand fork of the two improved tracks ahead. In about 125 yards turn left along a grassy forest track **(A)**. Upon reaching the end of this at a T-Junction, turn right along a gently ascending forest ride with conifers, left, and broadleaved trees, right.

Pignal & Ramnor Inclosures

Site Forestry Commission (FC)

Start Standing Hat

Parking FC Standing Hat car park

Public transport Brockenhurst station is just over ½ mile south of the Balmer Lawn Hotel from which Standing Hat is approximately 1 mile to the east. Bluestar route 6 bus service (Forest Bus) between Southampton and Lymington stops at Brockenhurst

Distance 2¾ miles (4.4km)

Terrain Forest tracks and rides

OS maps Landranger 196, Explorer OL22

GPS waypoints
Start SU 314 036
(A) SU 315 037
(B) SU 313 041
(C) SU 311 047
(D) SU 310 041

Refreshment Pubs and cafés in Brockenhurst

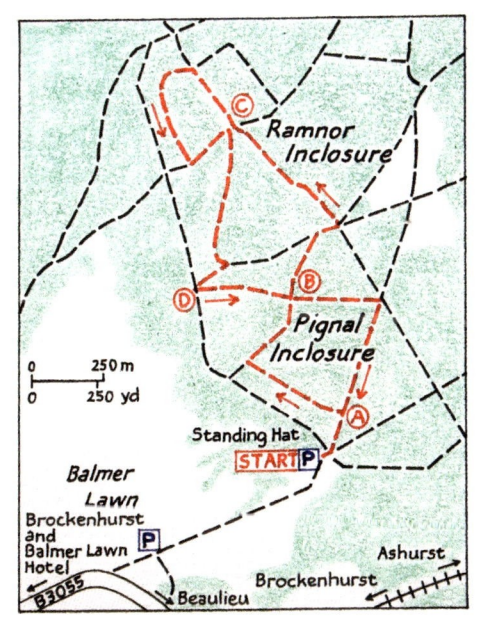

Climb to a track crossways **(B)** and go straight over. Continue ahead, gradually rising to intercept an improved stony track. Bear right along it to reach a sweeping right-hand bend and track junction. Leave the main track by walking ahead for a few paces and then turn left up a narrower ride. This rises gradually to meet the improved track/cycleway on a bend **(C)**. Walk straight over to the opposite track passing a felled trunk (left) of considerable girth. Stay with the track as it swings round to the left and where it next bends to the right, leave on the left along a narrower path, the tree cover noticeably more dense. This leads to a T-junction with a broader grassy ride; branch left, ascending to return to waypoint **(C)**.

This time fork right along the main track/cycleway *(watch out for speeding cyclists!)* following it downhill to arrive at a sweeping left-hand bend. Here turn right on to a narrower path, which shortly leads to a wider forest ride with a vehicle gateway on the right **(D)**. Turn sharp left; the track becomes more deeply rutted approaching the crossways **(B)**. Keep straight on here and walk out to meet the main forest track/cycleway once again. Turn right to return to Standing Hat.

Speckled Wood - above.
Pearl-bordered Fritillary - left

Ashley's picks
Brimstone – Apr to May; Aug to Sep
Small Tortoiseshell – Apr to May; Jul; Sep
Peacock – Apr to May; Aug to Sep
Speckled Wood – May to Jun; Aug to Sep
Pearl-bordered Fritillary – May

Walk 21 Hawkhill Inclosure and Beaulieu Heath

A lovely treat for high summer, where woodland and heathland butterflies intermingle along the forest fringes and clearings with ponies, dragonflies and Stonechats.

Many of the elements of a glorious New Forest landscape are encountered on this walk. There's Scots pine woodland, cleared forest of long grass and bracken, areas of well-grazed short turf, stands of oak and scattered birch, drainage ditches and boggy pools with attendant hawkers, trickling streams, woodland birdsong, dry heathland and carpets of heather (at its spectacular best in August), New Forest ponies, donkeys and cattle, Buzzards, Stonechats, Meadow Pipits and Skylarks, as well as aerobatic displays by model aircraft. Clouds of Silver-studded Blue make a memorable sight dancing over the drifts of purple Bell Heather. Grayling can usually be found on the heathland in front of Hawkhill Inclosure, White Admiral glide along the woodland rides and Dark Green Fritillary star in the open clearings.

The Walks
Hawkhill Inclosure loop
Go through the hand-gate at the rear of the car park. Branch left at a fork and soon bear left on to a main forest drive. Almost immediately, go straight over at a forest drive crossways – a post marking cycle route 344 is to the right – and settle in to enjoy a stroll through cleared and regenerating woodland. The stony drive sweeps right and very gently rises to a main junction of forest tracks **(A)**. Dark Green Fritillary can be seen in the clearing here and along the track for the next ½ mile.

Turn right. Keep ahead on the stony drive, pass a crossways with a grassy track and swing left with the main drive to reach a T-junction **(B)**. Go right (cycleway post 338); and the track leads you gently down to a bridge across Worts Gutter, rising through oak woodland on the other side.

Hawkhill Inclosure & Beaulieu Heath

At a T-junction the main track goes to the car park (right) but keep ahead on the narrower track passing through good White Admiral territory to reach a five-bar gate **(C)**. Silver-studded Blues favour the forest fringe to the left, while the car park lies to the right along the path edging Hawkhill Inclosure.

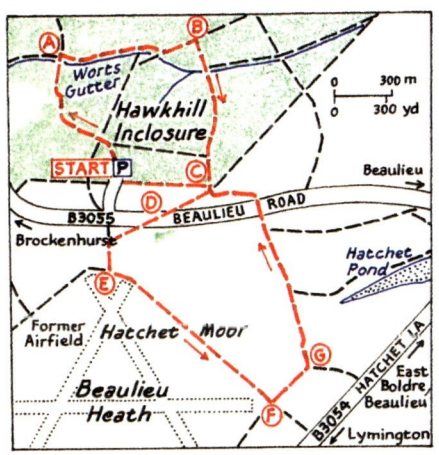

Beaulieu Heath loop

From **(C)**, walk forward a few paces and pick up a heathland path to the right, which delivers you to the main road **(D)** at the far edge of a Scots pine clump. Cross the B3055 diagonally to pick up the path and maintain the (C)-(D) direction. Turn left upon meeting a stony track coming from the main road and then left again at the old aerodrome taxiway **(E)**. Walk for just over ½ mile to the car park **(F)** off the B3054. About midway through the car park take the clear pony path off to the left, following a line of gorse to the left and with the chimneys of Fawley power station ahead in the distance. After about 250 yards take the left-hand path at a clear fork and very shortly intercept a crossing track **(G)**. Go left and soon, with Hatchet Pond visible to the right, walk down to cross the boggy ground around the lake's feeder stream. Once over this the way soon dries again; it picks up an ancient earthwork bank to the right, guiding you back to the B3055. Cross the main road and bear left, locating a path heading towards the gate at **(C)**. Here turn left and walk along the edge of Hawkhill Inclosure to return to the car park. The heath on either side of the car park driveway is a good spot for Grayling.

Site Hawkhill Inclosure: Forestry Commission (FC)

Parking Hawkhill Inclosure FC car park, off B3055, west of Hatchet Pond between Brockenhurst and Beaulieu

Public transport None

Distance Hawkhill Inclosure loop: 1½ miles (2.5km); Beaulieu Heath loop: 2½ miles (4.3km)

Terrain Hawkhill Inclosure loop: good, gently undulating forest tracks. Beaulieu Heath loop: flat heath, pony paths and old aerodrome taxiway

OS maps Landranger 196, Explorer OL22

GPS waypoints
Start SU 350 019
(A) SU 348 025
(B) SU 354 025
(C) SU 355 018
(D) SU 353 016
(E) SU 350 013
(F) SU 358 007
(G) SU 360 009

Refreshment Turfcutters Arms, East Boldre

Bell Heather – larval foodplant of Silver-studded Blue; female - left

Ashley's picks
Meadow Brown – Jun to Aug
Small Heath – Jun; Aug
Ringlet – Jul to Aug
Silver-studded Blue – Jul
Grayling – Aug

Walk 22 Walter's Copse and Newtown Meadows

Peaceful and seemingly timeless, this lovely woodland dates in fact from the mid-19th century on the edge of what was once the Island's busiest port.

The route described in Walter's Copse keeps to the wide rides, where much of the butterfly action is likely to be found. These are ribbons of ancient meadow that existed prior to the wood becoming established through the Victorian era. Here wildflowers provide a valuable nectar source for woodland and some grassland butterflies. The woodland is of oak and ash with an understorey of hazel coppice, which the National Trust still manages on a traditional 8-year cycle, principally to ensure a good supply of hazelnuts for the Red Squirrel and Dormouse populations. Discarded nibbled nutshells may be the only evidence you see of either species although if you are very quiet and very fortunate you may spot a Red Squirrel.

Newtown Meadows is a remnant of ancient hay meadow and looks its very best in spring. Before leaving it is worth seeing the Old Town Hall (see NT website for opening times).

The Walk

Leave the NT car park by the vehicle entrance and turn left along the lane. Bend with it to the right and walk on for about 700 yards to a NT sign and gateway to Walter's Copse **(A)**, where the lane bends sharply right. A short way before this on the left is the entrance to Town Copse (NT) and immediately prior to Walter's Copse is the entrance to Newtown National Nature Reserve.

Both these are worthwhile woodland wanders leading to Clamerkin Lake, a quiet backwater of the wetland wildlife paradise that is Newtown Harbour. *See alternative route on map from (B).*

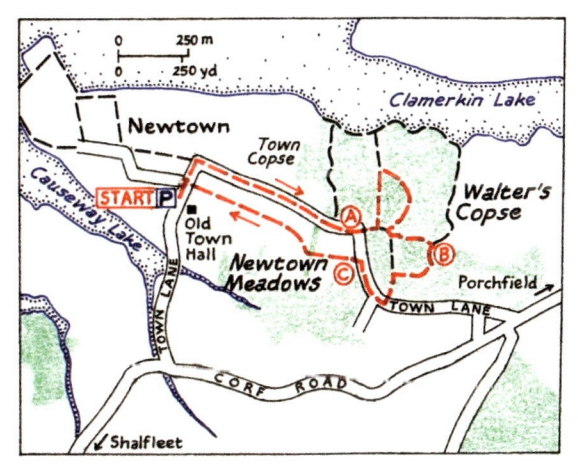

Pass the reserve's sightings board and keep ahead along the wide ride, shortly reaching a T-junction. Turn left. Soon the main track makes a long right-hand curve; the narrower path heading straight on into the coppice, just at the start of the bend, leads to Clamerkin Lake. Follow the main ride as it loops round to another T-junction. There are three options: to the right is the reserve gate (A), straight ahead the ride goes due south to reach a second reserve gate and NT sign (about 250 yards); or take a third option, left, to walk another loop of wide ride. Pass a turning on the left for a narrower path **(B)** and keep looping round to a track intersection and go left to reach the lane.

Turn right. Around the bend, look out for a finger-post and NT sign for Newtown Meadows **(C)**. Pass through the kissing-gate and follow the field path across the ancient meadow. After a strip of woodland the path continues through a waymarked hedge gap and crosses a field to a stile. Over this follow the trod to a gap at the end of the right-hand hedge, walk to and climb the waymarked stile, bear left and stride along a delightful green lane, once part of Newtown's High Street, enclosed by hedgerows. Pass through the kissing-gate at the end to return to the start.

Walter's Copse & Newtown Meadows

Site National Trust (NT)

Parking NT car park oppsite Newtown Old Town Hall. Alternatively, take the lane at the T-junction just north of the Old Town Hall and park at the end of the lane, past the church, for the bird hide.

Public transport Nearest available is Southern Vectis route 7 bus service to Shalfleet, from where it is approximately 1 mile to Newtown Old Town Hall.

Distance 1¾ miles (2.9km)

Terrain Lanes and woodland rides and paths

OS maps Landranger 196, Explorer OL29

GPS waypoints
Start SZ 423 906
(A) SZ 429 904
(B) SZ 432 904
(C) SZ 429 903

Refreshment Nearest, the New Inn at Shalfleet

Wych Elm – larval foodplant of White-letter Hairstreak - left; Comma

Ashley's picks
Comma – Apr; Jul; Sep
Holly Blue – Apr to May; Aug
Speckled Wood – May; Aug to Sep
White-letter Hairstreak – Jul
White Admiral – July to Aug

57

Walk 23 — Brook, Compton and Afton Downs

Not the highest points on the Island, but the superb mainland views and wildflower and butterfly profusion will leave you feeling on top of the world.

Walking out through the Compton Farm camping field in August, the impressive spine of high chalk downs raises levels of Lepidopteral anticipation. Passing through the entrance gate to Brook Down, there is an immediate transition into a butterfly-filled kaleidoscope of colour, the unimproved and wildflower-rich grassland on the lower slope of the down home to six species of Blue. In July the airy top of the ridge is more suited to the stronger flight of Dark Green Fritillary, while Kestrels, true masters of the air currents here, display their hovering prowess in good numbers. Brook merges into Compton Down and, while taking in the truly sumptuous views here, do watch out for waywardly driven golf balls before passing on to Afton Down. The descent towards the Military Road should be accompanied in season by Adonis, Chalkhill and Common Blues, Brown Argus and Clouded Yellow.

After leaving Afton Down on the last leg of the walk, in May/early June, look out for Glanville Fritillary on the crumbling cliffs of Compton Chine. Walk south along the cliff top and then down the wooden steps to the beach before making your way back to the parking area at Compton Farm.

Brook, Compton & Afton Downs

The Walk

Cross the cattle-grid and walk along the access track to Compton Farm. Pass the farm pond and cross a second cattle-grid, following the farm track left and then right past barns and outbuildings. Enter the campsite field, walking parallel to the hedgerow off to the right and with the impressive downland ridge ahead to the left. Continue across the field to a gateway **(A)** leading on to Brook Down, the approach of which is heralded by lots of butterfly activity.

Keep ahead along the chalky track. Look out to the left for butterflies on the down's lower slope, on the chalky bank of the track itself, and around the scrubby bushes lining the way. Pass two old chalk pits (at SZ 382 851 and SZ 385 851), the sheltered microclimates of which host a shimmering tableau of butterflies. Behind you, the eye-catching line of chalk cliffs rim Freshwater Bay. Eventually reach a pair of gateposts **(B)** and, about 50 yards beyond, bear left, rising to pass around the head of a cattle pen scooped from the hillside. Walk on to intercept a prominent chalk track rising from the right and turn uphill along it.

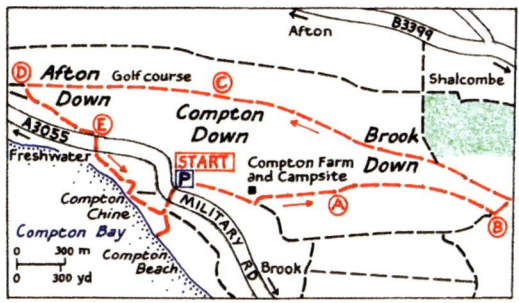

Rise to the ridge line of Brook Down and delight in the panorama. Stay on the turf carpet, drawing you onward past a crater (SZ 381 854) and over Compton Down to arrive at a hand-gate **(C)** giving on to the Freshwater Bay Golf Course. Now on Afton Down, continue along the ridge and at the end of the golf course turn left **(D)**, cutting the corner behind the last of the greens and bunkers. Soon reach a path, go left and descend Afton Down to the Military Road **(E)**. Cross the road and turn left, walking along the verge to reach a stile and fingerpost on the right. Over the stile follow the path across Compton Chine to a kissing-gate opposite the Compton Farm car park.

Site mostly National Trust (NT)

Parking NT car park off the A3055, Military Road, at Compton Farm

Public transport Southern Vectis route 12 bus service; bus stop adjacent to car park and Compton Farm access track

Distance 4¼ miles (7km)

Terrain Chalk track, downland and field paths, and golf course fairway. Moderate ascents

OS maps Landranger 196, Explorer OL29

GPS waypoints
Start SZ 370 851
(A) SZ 381 851
(B) SZ 389 850
(C) SZ 373 856
(D) SZ 361 856
(E) SZ 364 854

Refreshment Seasonal ice cream van in Compton Chine and/or Compton Down car parks

Clover – larval foodplant of Clouded Yellow; Wall Brown - left

Ashley's picks
Wall Brown – May; Aug
Small Blue – May to Jun; Aug
Adonis Blue – May to Jun; Aug to Sep
Chalkhill Blue – Jul to Aug
Grayling – Aug

Walk 24 | Tennyson Down

High on this lofty down, a chance to follow in Tennyson's footsteps and watch, as it is said he often did, 'the sunlight glint on butterfly's wings'.

Originally called East High Down, it was renamed in Tennyson's honour. The memorial, erected in 1897 after the poet's death, is on the highest point of the down, 147m (482ft) above sea level. The bench, half way up the climb towards the monument, is the perfect place to sit and observe soaring seabirds, catch the interplay of light and water over the English Channel or, perhaps, of a warm summer's evening, to watch the setting sun sink beyond Headon Warren which, out of sight, leads to the Needles.

According to the National Trust, Tennyson Down came fourth in a nationwide survey to determine the best places to picnic in Britain. It is high, too, on any list of the best spots to observe blue butterflies, especially Adonis, Chalkhill and Common Blues. The old quarry, partly used as a car park, and hummocky 'waste' ground to the left of the old track leading to the foot of the down, have longer grass, trees and scrubby shelter making alternative habitat to the close-cropped downland carpet on the open slopes of Tennyson Down. The descent on the north slope of the down is mostly through ash woodland and Brimstone, Speckled Wood, Gatekeeper and Holly Blue can be found along the hedge-lined path, initially stepped, back to the car park.

Tennyson Down

The Walk

From the car park entrance, facing downhill, turn left past a low barrier to walk along a chalky path. Pass an information board and a sign 'permissive horse path, no galloping'. Glimpses of the chalk pit can be seen on the left. Pass through a hand-gate and keep ahead. The track leads on to a meeting of ways **(A)** in front of a beacon and, beyond this, a fence and gateway.

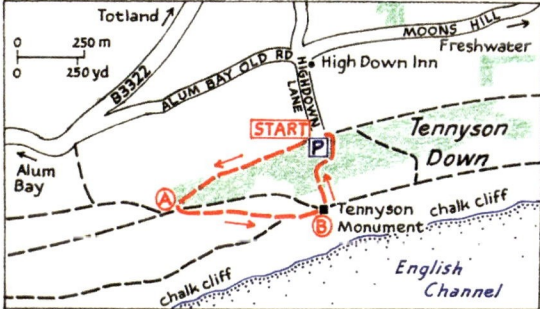

Here turn left, following the broad turf carpet up the slope towards Tennyson's Monument, which marks the top of the climb. There's a bench mid-climb from which to gaze westwards across the down and watch the busyness of butterflies and other insects going about their business over this finest of chalk grasslands. At the monument **(B)**, after taking in the epic views, leave with your back to the cross and the sea behind you, heading north, down the slope towards scrub and bushes with Totland ahead and Hurst Castle, seemingly perilously placed mid-Solent, leading your eye on to the mainland. Pick up a more discernible path through the scrub, which leads on to some steps as the more purposeful descent begins. Stay with this path through a kissing-gate and reach a NT sign at the bottom. To the left the path picks a way around the edge of the chalk pit to return to the car park.

Site National Trust (NT)

Parking NT car park in the old chalk pit at the end of Highdown Lane

Public transport Southern Vectis route 7 bus service to Alum Bay and Needles Breezer, and Island Coaster services stop at the Highdown Inn

Distance 1 mile (1.7km)

Terrain Chalk down paths and tracks. Moderate ascents and descents

OS maps Landranger 196, Explorer OL29

GPS waypoints
Start SZ 324 856
(A) SZ 319 853
(B) SZ 324 853

Refreshment The Highdown Inn, Totland, at the foot of the lane leading up to the NT car park

Common Rockrose – larval foodplant of Brown Argus. Brown Argus and Chalkhill Blues - left

Ashley's picks
Large Skipper – Jun to Aug
Small Skipper – Jun to Aug
Brown Argus – May to Jun; Aug to Sep
Dark Green Fritillary – Jul
Small Heath – Jun; Aug to Sep

Walk 25 Bonchurch Down and Wheeler's Bay

Bonchurch Down is a steep chalk hillside luxuriant in wildflowers and butterflies; the crumbling cliffs of Wheeler's Bay are a Glanville stronghold.

'Last, but not least' is an apt expression for this energetic circuit around Ventnor; the last walk in this guide links two sites of exceptional Lepidopteral interest. It can also be enjoyed as two separate walks, cutting out the more arduous climbing and slippery descents *and the best option for vertigo sufferers*, by making the routes a there-and-back across Bonchurch Down and an easy stroll along the promenade from Ventnor.

Bonchurch Down, part of the National Trust's Ventnor Downs property, rises steeply behind the town. Old English goats graze the down to keep the scrub at bay. Glorious spreads of Horseshoe Vetch support a good population of Adonis Blue.

Wheeler's Bay, south-east facing over the English Channel, is a good spot to see immigrant butterflies such as Painted Lady and Clouded Yellow. The walk follows the Isle of Wight Coast Path along the concrete seawall skirting the cliff base. It was built in the 1990s to protect against coastal erosion, a measure that, controversially for Glanville colonies, reduces the number of regular cliff falls relied upon for growth of Ribwort Plantain, their main larval foodplant.

The Walk
Cross the A3055 *with care* and pass through the hand-gate, waymarked V123 Luccombe Down. Do not take this steeply climbing path, but fork left on a narrower grassy trod across the bottom of the slope. Edging a line of trees it reaches a kissing-gate **(A)** leading on to Bonchurch Down.

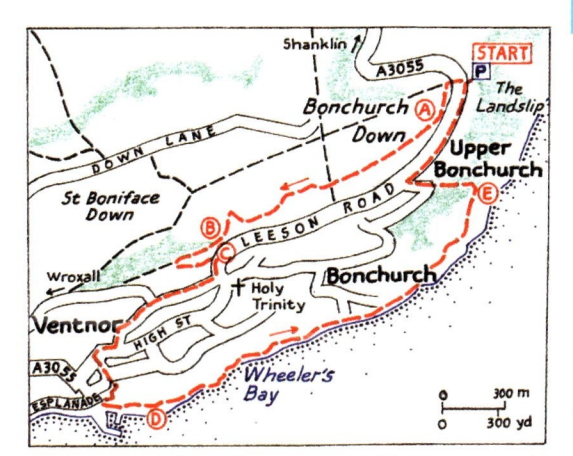

Bonchurch Down & Wheeler's Bay

Site Bonchurch Down, National Trust (NT)

Parking The Landslip parking area and information point, on the south side of the A3055 on the edge of Upper Bonchurch, Ventnor

Public transport Southern Vectis route 3 bus service from Ryde; nearest stop at The Landslip parking area

Distance 4 miles (6.8km)

Terrain Uneven grassy path across Bonchurch Down followed by a steep and slippery descent through Holm Oak woodland; pavement through Ventnor; concrete walkway along the undercliff between Wheeler's Bay and Monks Bay; steep and uneven climb up the cliff to return to the start

OS maps Landranger 196, Explorer OL29

GPS waypoints
Start SZ 580 788
(A) SZ 579 786
(B) SZ 569 781
(C) SZ 568 780
(D) SZ 566 773
(E) SZ 579 780

Take care with foot placement on this uneven path, contouring across the steeply-sloping down above the back gardens of Bonchurch, below on the left. There's a succession of dips and rises and a wonderful view over the spire of Ventnor church. At length, reach a kissing-gate and NT sign **(B)**. Pass through to descend across the slope under a dense canopy of Holm Oak woodland. At the bottom go left through a kissing-gate and follow the path to another kissing-gate and NT sign: the entrance to St Boniface Down **(C)**. Turn right along the main road and first right into St Boniface Road, B3327. Bear left at a road sign for the Esplanade/Town Centre. Meeting the High Street turn right, follow it left in front of The Blenheim pub, then keep left into Pier Street. Keep ahead, descending through public seafront gardens to a car park entrance. Turn left.

At the end of the car park **(D)** go past a vehicle barrier and walk along the concrete apron with towering chalk cliffs on the left. Eventually reach a Glanville mosaic in the wall, produced by Ventnor School in 2013. Past the last property on the left, take the cliff path beginning the climb back to the start. Initially, keep to the lower path and, later, at a junction **(E)** marked 'Coast Path' to the right, turn left. Pass through an old wooden kissing gate, climb some eroded steps and, shortly after some wooden steps, emerge on a lane at a hairpin bend. Continue uphill to the main road, turn right to reach the Smugglers Haven tearoom and, just beyond, The Landslip parking area.

Ribwort Plantain - larval foodplant of Glanville Fritillary - left

Glanville Fritillary

Ashley's picks
Glanville Fritillary – May to Jun
Adonis Blue – May to Jun; Aug to Sep
Clouded Yellow – May to Sep
Dingy Skipper – May to Jun
Wall Brown – May; Aug

Butterfly Flight Periods

Orange denotes main flight period; monthly divisions are simplified into 4-weekly periods.

	March 1 2 3 4	April 1 2 3 4	May 1 2 3 4	June 1 2 3 4	July 1 2 3 4	August 1 2 3 4	September 1 2 3 4	October 1 2 3 4
Red Admiral								
Painted Lady								
Small White								
Small Tortoiseshell								
Peacock								
Brimstone								
Comma								
Holly Blue								
Green-veined White								
Speckled Wood								
Clouded Yellow								
Large White								
Small Copper								
Orange-tip								
Green Hairstreak								
Grizzled Skipper								
Wall Brown								
Duke of Burgundy								
Common Blue								
Pearl-bordered Fritillary								
Dingy Skipper								
Glanville Fritillary								
Brown Argus								
Small Blue								
Small Heath								
Adonis Blue								
Marsh Fritillary								
Small Pearl-bordered Fritillary								
Large Skipper								
Meadow Brown								
Small Skipper								
Dark Green Fritillary								
Marbled White								
Ringlet								
White Admiral								
Silver-studded Blue								
White-letter Hairstreak								
Silver-washed Fritillary								
Gatekeeper								
Purple Emperor								
Chalkhill Blue								
Purple Hairstreak								
Essex Skipper								
Grayling								
Silver-spotted Skipper								
Brown Hairstreak